D0615310

The Cognitive Basis of the Intellect:

A Response to Jensen's "Bias in Mental Testing"

Sonja C. Grover

University of Calgary
Calgary, Alberta

Copyright © 1981 by

University Press of America, Inc.

P.O. Box 19101, Washington, D.C. 20036

Library of Congress Cataloging in Publication Data

Grover, Sonja C.
    The cognitive basis of the intellect.

    Includes index.
    1. Jensen, Arthur Robert. Bias in mental testing
2. Intelligence tests. 3. Intellect. 4. Cognition
5. Minorities--Testing. I. Jensen, Arthur Robert.
Bias in mental testing. II. Title.
BF432.A1J4634   153.9'3   81-40303
ISBN 0-8191-1741-2   AACR2
ISBN 0-8191-1742-0 (pbk.)

To my parents and Roshan

ACKNOWLEDGEMENTS

I wish to express my gratitude to my parents who conveyed to me something of their respect for the individual's right to define himself via his actions, free from prejudgements, stereotypes, stigmatizing labels and arbitrary classification schemes. Such a perspective was essential to the writing of this book which is in part an argument against the restriction of choices and denial of educational, vocational or other opportunities on the basis of psychometric test scores.

To my husband, Roshan, I extend my sincere thanks for his constant emotional support and encouragement. It is he who saw the potential for a book while listening to my mutterings about the inadequacies and abuses of current mental tests as well as promising research trends in the area.

In addition, I thank my father for his skilful and enthusiastic proof-reading of the entire manuscript.

CONTENTS

PREFACE

The objective of this text is to bring to the fore some of the faulty assumptions regarding cognitive process underlying many widely used mental tests. It will be argued that the tests are in large part based on assumptions which are logically flawed and inconsistent with much of the evidence in current cognitive and neuropsychological research.

Suggestions for a more humane and empirically sound approach to mental testing are developed.

It is suggested further, in contrast to Jensen's view, that mental tests are seriously biased against certain minority groups in that racial group differences in mental test scores do not reflect fundamental differences in cognitive process nor of intellect. Nevertheless, these tests continue to be used for selection purposes and hence block social mobility, for black minorities in particular. The question of why and to what degree such tests predict socially relevant variables takes on new meaning; given that the tests do not measure significant aspects of brain function.

Jensen's claim that major mental tests such as the WISC and various nonverbal mental measures assess "thinking" skills is examined in the light of empirical evidence from the cognitive literature, and discredited.

Finally, the question of what has been learned as the result of the errors made by the promulgators of the mental testing movement is considered. The errors, it is suggested, hold some important inadvertent lessons for the researcher, practitioner and public at large regarding the practical consequences of naive philosophies of science.

INTRODUCTION

Overview of Jensen's Position and Style of Argumentation

Intelligence Identified with the g Factor

Jensen argues that intelligence can be identified with the g factor "of an indefinitely large and varied battery of mental tests" (1, p. 249). The g factor itself is held to be a "hypothetical construct not itself directly measurable" (2, pp. 223-234). It is a factor involved in diverse mental abilities and is not itself an ability but rather as Wechsler put it and Jensen concurs "a property of mind" (3, p. 124).

According to Jensen, "It makes little sense to say that g is more an aspect of tests than of persons . . . The common elements (of diverse test items) are something in the brain, not in the test items as such" (4, p. 236).

In Jensen's view, mental measures that are highly "g loaded" measure significant cognitive processes and not "merely knowledge and skills acquired in a school or in a cultured home" (5, p. 364). Tests which are highly g loaded, according to Jensen, tend to measure higher level skills such as : "mental manipulation of input, " " choice," "decision," "invention," "meaningful memory," and "long term memory," as opposed to rote activities requiring less conscious and complex mental processing (6, p. 250). In sum, these tests, according to Jensen, measure thinking and the processes underlying intelligent behavior. Jensen cites Bereiter's informal definition of intelligence as "What you do when you don't know what to do' (7, p. 232) and implies that highly g loaded tests tap such processes.

In Jensen's view, intelligence and consequently the g factor, is more than simply a set of cognitive strategies, the latter being but a manifestation of the intellect. "To mistake cognitive strategies themselves for g is to confuse cause and effect" (8, p. 246) according to Jensen. The acquisition of cognitive strategies and "superstrategies" for the monitoring of lower level strategies and invention of new ones is, Jensen claims, an ability which is "itself highly g loaded" (9,p. 246).

Hence, while unable to specify directly the nature of g itself, Jensen argues that we are today "far from being totally in the dark concerning the nature of what intelligence tests measure." (10, p. 173).

Mental Tests as Neutral, Independent Measures
of "Real" Individual and Group Differences

Jensen holds that mental tests are neutral devices which can be used to assess differences between individuals and groups which exist in nature and are not but a function of the measuring devices themselves. He states, "Tests only reveal differences, they neither create them nor explain their causes . . . The observed racial group differences are real in the sense that they are not merely an artifact of the measuring instruments" (11, p. 737).

Jensen further contends that discriminatory practices and criteria are matters of social policy and do not follow automatically "from the power of tests to discriminate" (12, p. 44). Hence, in his view, abolishing tests would *not* inevitably lead to fairer selection procedures and just treatment for minority groups. Nor would the differences between racial groups and between individuals which mental tests highlight disappear were mental tests done away with. Such problematic differences in intellectual functioning, Jensen asserts, would continue despite abolition of the measuring devices which detect them. This claim leads Jensen to comment wryly, "One cannot treat a fever by throwing away the thermometer" (13, p. xi).

As to the causes of such individual and group differences Jensen states that test constructors, publishers and users "can remain agnostic on that issue"(14, p. 740).

Human Intelligence Varies More so According to Brain Structure Than as a Function of How the Person Uses His Brain

Jensen cites the evidence of Van Valen who claims that brain size and intellect are causally related with larger brain size presumably being related to more complex intellectual functioning (15). Earlier in his text, he refers to Cyril Burt's notion that "complexity in the neural architecture" is related to the g factor (16).

He implies that intelligence is somehow causally related to brain structure and not simply a function of how the brain processes information., He rejects the view that "there are no individual differences in the brain itself but only differences in how persons use their brains" (17, p. 245), a view he attributes to those who hold that intelligence is but a matter of learned strategies.

Mental Tests as a Means to a More Democratic Society

Jensen contends that as mental tests "are more impersonal and yet more individual and objective" (18, p. 49) than other methods of selection they ought to be retained. In his view, objective tests in educational and employment selection have promoted social justice. "The application of sound psychometrics," Jensen contends, "can eliminate unfair

3

treatment based on sex, race, social class, religion or national origin" (19, p. 740). Jensen flatly rejects the view that mental tests are biased against minority groups and holds instead that they have served to enhance social mobility for most, if not all, such groups (the notable exception being black Americans).

Critics of Mental Testing are Non-Empirical, Armchair Philosophers with Insecure Personalities

According to Jensen, test critics are non-empirical types whose criticisms of testing seem to "convey attitudes and sentiments instead of information that would be needed to evaluate arguments" (20, p. 18). He speaks of an "antitest syndrome" (21, p. 18) and cites Brim who characterized anti-test individuals as hostile to self-examination, introspection or self-understanding (22, p. 21). Jensen attributes also to such individuals the view that "important human attributes cannot be measured or dealt with quantitatively or understood in any scientifically meaningful sense" (23, p. 18).

Jensen's Position Challenged

The attempt in this text is to address each of the aforementioned assumptions using both logical arguments and empirical evidence, Below are listed Jensen's assumptions and the chapters which deal most directly with each:

Assumptions   **Chapters**

(a) Intelligence as the g Factor 2, 4, 11

Jensen's assumptions regarding the heritability of intelligence and the notion that "the extent to which any test measures genetically conditioned factors can be determined via the methods of quantitative genetics" (24, p. 9) will not be discussed as this topic has already been most skillfully dealt with by various authors such as Kamin (25). The focus in this text will instead be upon the inadequacy of current mental tests in assessing basic cognitive processes.

This author is not arguing that such basic cognitive processes are inherently immeasurable, contrary to what Jensen claims an opponent of current mental testing practices would generally hold. Evidence will be presented from the cognitive and neuropsychological literature to demonstrate that most mental tests are designed without consideration of the empirical findings of this literature, but instead according to principles of convenience and social expediency, and are therefore importantly lacking in construct validity.

Issues of "fairness" and "unfairness," it will be suggested, are valid considerations for the scientist, issues which lead to no more debate on metaphysical topics than do discussions regarding test design and what it is mental tests measure.

Jensen holds that issues of fairness and unfairness must be avoided in scientific circles; to be replaced by "utilitarian considerations"

5

which are "more amenable to objective analysis with the techniques of psychometrics and statistics" (26, p. 49). However, if it is asked as it must be, "utilitarian from whose point of view, and according to which criteria?", then one enters again into philosophical debate. The answers to such questions are not to be found in statistical charts but may be discovered by examination of the aspirations of and choices available to individuals.

REFERENCES

1. Jensen, A. R. *Bias in Mental Testing.* New York: The Free Press, 1980, p. 249.

2. Ibid, p. 233-234.

3. Wechsler, D. *Manual for the Wechsler Intelligence Scale for Children* (Revised). New York: Psychological Corporation, 1974.

4. Jensen, A. R. *Bias in Mental Testing,* p. 236.

5. Ibid., p. 364.

6. Ibid., p. 250.

7. Ibid., p. 232.

8. Ibid., p. 246.

9. Ibid.

10. Ibid., p. 173.

11. Ibid., p. 737.

12. Ibid., p. 44.

13. Ibid., p. xi.

14. Ibid., p. 740.

15. Van Valen, L. Brain size and intelligence in man. *American Journal of Physical Anthropology,* 1974, 40, p. 417-423.

16. Burt, C. Factor analysis and its neurological basis. *British Journal of Mathematical and Statistical Psychology,* 1961, 14, p. 53-71.

17. Jensen, A. R. *Bias in Mental Testing,* p. 245.

18. Ibid., p. 49.

19. Ibid., p. 740.

20. Ibid., p. 18.

21. Ibid.

22. Brim, O.G., Jr. American attitudes towards intelligence tests. *American Psychologist,* 1965, 20, pp. 125-130.

23. Jensen, A. R. *Bias in Mental Testing,* p. 18.

24. Ibid., p. 9.

25. Kamin, L. J. *The Science and Politics of I.Q.* New York: Penguin Books, 1974.

26. Jensen, A.R. *Bias in Mental Testing,* p. 49.

PART I

ASSUMPTIONS UNDERLYING MENTAL TESTS WHICH REQUIRE REVISION

CHAPTER ONE

FAULTY ASSUMPTIONS REGARDING COGNITIVE PROCESS

Intelligence, in Jensen's view, can be identified with the g factor. Further, an examination of what types of items result in tests being highly loaded on the g factor, Jensen assumes, provides insights into what cognitive process such mental tests measure and into the nature of intelligence itself.

It is here suggested that such an examination of test items does not suffice to reveal whether or not they measure anything significant about cognitive process at all. If these items have predictive validity (a topic which will be discussed in further detail later) to assume that such predictive validity automatically serves to verify one's conceptual model of the hypothetical brain processes tapped by the test items is to commit a serious logical error known as "affirming the consequent."[1]

Difficulties in Determining What
Mental Test Items Measure

Jensen assumes, among other things, that whether a task measures primarily verbal or nonverbal processes can be readily determined as can the degree of culture-loading of the task(s). In addition, he suggests that "the specific content of items is unessential . . . the content is a mere vehicle for the essential elements of intelligence test items" (1, p. 127). Timed tests, Jensen claims, do not measure variables extraneous to what the test was intended to measure such as intelligence, if one assures that the subjects' rank order would be the same despite variations in time limits afforded subjects writing the test. These claims are examined in what follows.

Verbal versus Nonverbal Items

In response to the aforementioned claims it can be said that distinctions between verbal and nonverbal tasks cannot be made in any but the most imprecise and general fashion in that both may depend on fundamentally similar cognitive processing depending on the specifics of the task.

Consider certain of the so-called "performance" subtests of the Wechsler Scale: picture arrangement, digit symbol and block design. The picture arrangement subtest involves arranging cartoon pictures in a logical sequence. It is quite likely that competence on this task is importantly related to ability in generating covert, analytical, verbal descriptions of alternative story sequences which serve to guide the individual's picture arrangements.

Digit symbol is also classed as a performance or nonverbal task. This subtest requires the subject to translate the numerals 1 to 9 into symbols according to a code, where the digits are listed in random order in several rows. Covert verbalization may be involved in this subtest as a means of making sense of the novel code symbols. For instance, the subject may store the symbol as "a triangle with the bottom missing." The adequacy of such covert, verbal descriptions of the symbols and ability of subjects to store these descriptions may determine efficiency on the task. Novel, memorable verbal descriptions of the symbol may allow subjects to match symbols with numbers without having to constantly recheck the code provided at the top of the response sheet.

Since this subtest is timed, if covert verbalization were to facilitate recall of the code, the total subtest score would be significantly affected as a result.

Block design is a subtest in which subjects are required to duplicate a series of cards displaying two-dimensional red and white designs using a set of one-inch wooden cubes painted red and white. Internal verbal descriptions of the two-dimensional displays may be quite relevant to this task and may guide manipulation of the three-dimensional blocks.

That subjects often rely upon covert verbal labelling and more elaborate verbal descriptions in tasks involving recall of nonverbal items is a well established finding (2). Whether such covert verbalization enhances or hinders performance seems to depend on a number of task specific variables (3, 4). The point of issue here, however, is the impossibility of drawing clear demarcation lines between verbal and nonverbal items.

Not only do subjects often invoke covert verbalizations while doing so-called nonverbal tasks but they often call upon spatial images in certain kinds of verbal reasoning tasks (5).

Studies such as those of Brooks (6) have demonstrated that formulating internal spatial or verbal representations may involve common sensory channels in certain tasks. For instance, Brooks was able to induce conflict when subjects were required to simultaneously read messages and visualize the spatial relations described in those messages. "Hence reading interferes with the generation of an internal representation of spatial relations" (7, p. 145). To assume that subjects rely only on verbal processing when a task is labelled as a verbal one or but spatial imagery when the task is regarded as composed of performance items is to grossly oversimplify the cognitive processes involved.

The Cultural-Loading of Items

Jensen himself concedes that "there is remarkably little variation in any group's mean score, in relation to majority norms, across the more and less culture-reduced tests" (8, p. 642). Of course, Jensen attributes this finding to factors other than the possibility that so-called culture-reduced tests are not significantly culture-reduced in fact.

In Jensen's view, performance tests, tests with nonverbal content, and familiar item content, tests involving abstract reasoning, and nonscholastic skills are more culture-reduced than are paper and pencil tests with verbal items or those involving unfamiliar content and academic skills (9, p. 637). There exists a body of research, however, which clearly contradicts the view that test content is culture-reduced simply because it is nonverbal, nonacademic or presents novel problems. One study belonging to this literature is that of Wagner (10).

Wagner compared the performance of urban and rural schooled and nonschooled Moroccans and Koranic school students on memory tasks involving little verbal response. Subjects were required to recall the serial position of a particular line drawing on a card after presentation briefly (2 sec.) of seven drawings which were placed in front of the subjects. On this *pictorial* recall task, urban schooled subjects demonstrated a greater primacy effect[2] than did the rural schooled, followed by the urban unschooled subjects, and the rural unschooled subjects, respectively. In other words, extent of schooling and environmental (urban vs rural) experience can have a dramatic effect on tasks which involve pictorial items and therefore, according to Jensen's criteria, fall into the culture-reduced category. Wagner further found that the urban environment was sufficient for effective short-term memory performance for younger subjects on this task, with the effects of schooling increasing for those over age 13. The increase in primacy in the schooled group suggests that "verbally mediated rehearsal strategies are more available" to older schooled children" (11, p. 13).

Wagner's second study in the same series turned up findings which contradict the notion that familiar item content leads to a more culture-reduced test than does less familiar item content. Wagner contrasted the performance of Moroccan rug sellers and Michigan psychology students in addition to the groups in the first study on a recognition task. The task involved presentation of 207 photographs of Oriental rugs. Subjects were to specify which items had appeared previously in the list. Significant effects for schooling and environment were again obtained with rural, nonschooled subjects performing better than schooled, urban subjects. Wagner rejects the interpretation that subjects in rural areas were more familiar with the patterns as the rugs are widely available in both urban and rural areas in Morocco. Hence, these nonschooled children were adept at recognizing complex patterns while performing poorly with much simpler pictorial material on a short-term serial recall task.

Even more striking was the finding that Michigan university students, unfamiliar with the patterns of Oriental rugs, performed better on this task than did the rug sellers or rural subjects. Wagner suggests this superiority might have been a function of the American students' schooling.

These findings seem to imply that the cognitive strategies which are developed via schooling are brought into play even when item content is nonverbal and/or familiar. One must concur with Wagner that his work illustrates "the complex nature of the relationships between particular tasks, particular cognitive skills and particular aspects of culture" (12, p. 22). It seems naive then to assume that merely ensuring pictorial content and familiar material, for example, will necessarily reduce the culture-loading of the mental test.

Jensen claims that the item content of mental tests is irrelevant as long as it is apprehended in the same way by all persons taking the test. This principle is termed the "indifference of the indicator" (13, p. 127). It seems clear from Wagner's study, however, that all test items are *not* encoded in the same way by all subjects. The same test items may trigger very different cognitive strategies depending on the experience of the individual taking the test, even when those items are nonverbal and, hence, allegedly culture-reduced.

Assessing "Pure" Intellect

Jensen appears to assume that it is possible to assess intelligence uncontaminated by factors of temperament. Thus he claims that timed tests pose no special problems by introducing extraneous variables into the measurement of the intellect as long as subjects' rank order remains constant despite variations in time limits assigned a test.

It is here argued, in contrast, that all mental measures, whether timed or untimed, are seriously contaminated by factors relating to the emotional make-up of the individual. Such emotional factors have a profound effect upon the individual's approach to solving problems, his

16

ability to make selections among alternatives, and the general efficiency of his information processing.

What is here suggested is that the fact that a test is timed may itself affect outcome as the result of effects mediated by both cognitive and emotional variables. Individuals may differ in terms of their susceptibility to such factors. Hence, rank order may change for some when the test is timed and not for others. For instance, locus of control (e.g., the degree to which one feels in control of outcomes) has been found to significantly affect problem solving performance. Individuals who are more internal in orientation (persons experiencing a sense of mastery) as opposed to external (lacking in a sense of control over the situation) have been found to be more efficient information processors (14). It is quite possible that timed tests would further exacerbate the external's sense of lack of control and so hinder performance. It is noteworthy that a number of studies have revealed that minority groups — Blacks, Spanish Americans, Indians and others — are more external in their orientation (15).

Speed and adequacy of performance under timed conditions, then, most likely are importantly influenced by emotional variables. For instance, certain timed tests may reinforce the problem of the overfocused, compulsive, and anxious child. Kinsbourne notes, for instance, that:

> On intelligence and achievement tests, overfocused children are likely to lose time credits. Given unlimited time, however, they do better . . . on WISC subtests like coding, one may observe the overfocuser carefully checking and rechecking each answer before moving to the next. On WISC Similarities and Comprehension

questions they may slowly but compulsively give lengthy detailed responses that go beyond the information requested (16, p. 284). Furthermore, efficient use of time appears to be profoundly affected by the individual's sense of mastery in tasks perceived to require certain skills. Internals have been found to take longer in making decisions under instructions which emphasize that the task outcome is dependent on skill than when instructions emphasize outcome is determined by chance. Externals show the reverse trend, being more deliberate with "chance" instructions, though the trend was not significant (17).

It is inappropriate that Jensen implies, as he seems to, that cognitive variables can be assessed apart from emotional factors in timed or untimed test situations. In this regard, a statement of Donald Norman's seems quite apropos: "It may well be that it is the cognitive component that is subservient . . . working through the emotions, through affect" (18, p. 1). Hence, emotional factors may, in large part, determine problem solving skills and style. Such appears to be a likely interpretation of studies such as that by Bloom (19). Bloom investigated the problem solving styles of high and low aptitude college students. He discovered that the poor students tended to adopt a very impulsive approach to problem solving in which the questions to be addressed were not fully understood before the student attempted the problem. Asked to reread questions, these students seemed quite competent at then understanding their implications. Also, these low aptitude students tended to have difficulty dealing with logical form and responded to syllogistic type reasoning problems often in terms of personal and emotional preferences and biases. What is of special interest is the fact that remedial training focusing upon more efficient problem solving strategies significantly affected performance in both the experimental setting and nonexperimental, with considerable increases in college grades resulting from the training program.

Aspects of cognitive style and temperament appear then to have considerable effect upon efficiency of information processing. It would seem that standard psychometric tests are as much a measure of such temperamental factors as of basic cognitive capacity, if indeed they are measures of the latter at all.

Whether the test is timed or untimed, it appears that emotional temperament is an important mediator of performance and, hence, of the score obtained. All mental tests are in essence timed, in any case, in the sense that the subjects being tested are usually quite aware that the tester is waiting for a response and will not provide unlimited time. There is, then, an implicit psychological pressure exerted to respond relatively rapidly and to move on to the next item despite one's insecurities regarding a previous response, for the assessment situation involves playing a game by someone else's rules.

In the next chapter are considered certain of the erroneous assumptions regarding the neural mechanisms underlying performance on psychometric tests which Jensen and others who favor his views on these issues have advanced.

REFERENCES

1. Jensen, A. R. *Bias in Mental Testing.* New York: The Free Press, 1980, p. 127.

2. Clark, H. J. Recognition memory for random shapes as a function of complexity, association value and delay. *Journal of Experimental Psychology,* 1965, 69, p. 590-595.

3. Vanderplas, J. M. and Garvin, E. A. Complexity, association value and practice as factors in shape recognition. *Journal of Experimental Psychology,* 1959, 57, p. 155-163.

4. Wilgosh, L. R. The interaction between pictures and their labels in the memory of four-year-old children. Unpublished doctoral dissertation, McMaster University, 1970.

5. Huttenlocher, J. Constructing spatial images: A strategy in reasoning. *Psychological Review,* 1968, 75, p 550 560.

6. Brooks, L. R. The suppression of visualization in reading. *Quarterly Journal of Experimental Psychology.* 1967, 9, p. 289-299.

7. Paivio, A. *Imagery and Verbal Processes.* New York: Holt, Rinehart and Winston Inc., 1971.

8. Jensen, A. R. *Bias in Mental Testing,* p. 642.

9. Ibid., p. 637.

10. Wagner, D. A. Memories of Morocco: The influence of age, schooling and environment on memory. *Cognitive Psychology,* 1978, 10, p. 1-28.

11. Ibid., p. 13.

12. Ibid., p. 22.

13. Jensen, A. R. *Bias in Mental Testing,* p. 127.

14. Lefcourt, H. M. *Locus of Control.* New York: John Wiley and Sons, 1976, p. 51-65.

15. ibid., p. 15-25.

16. Kinsbourne, M. and Caplan, P. J. *Children's Learning and Attention Problems.* Boston: Little, Brown and Company, 1979.

17. Rotter, J. B. and Mulry, R. Internal versus external control of reinforcements and decision time. *Journal of Personality and Social Psychology,* 1965, 2, p. 598-604.

18. Norman, D. A. Twelve issues for cognitive science. *Cognitive Science,* 1980, 4, 1-32.

19. Bloom, B. S. and Broder, T. *Problem-Solving Processes of College Students.* Chicago: University of Chicago Press, 1950.

NOTES

1. "Affirming the consequent" refers to the logical error of reasoning that a true consequent necessarily implies a true premise. Mahoney contends that "reasoning used in theory evaluation is often the illicit form of affirming the consequent" (1, p. 139) as when the scientist concludes that accurate predictions ipso facto verify the hypothesis upon which they were based.

2. The "primacy effect" refers to the phenomenon of remembering initial items in a serial list better than middle items. This is taken to be evidence for rehearsal of list items.

REFERENCE

1. Mahoney, M. *The Scientist as Subject: The Psychological Imperative,* Cambridge: Ballinger, 1976.

CHAPTER TWO

FAULTY ASSUMPTIONS REGARDING NEUROLOGICAL PROCESS

The Brain as an "All Purpose Computer" Reflected by the g Factor

Jensen argues that since transfer of strategy training tends to be quite narrow for individuals scoring poorly on I.Q. tests, explanations of intelligence in terms of learned strategies are inadequate. The g factor he takes to be separable, and the determiner of degree of transfer (1, p. 246).

Neurological evidence clearly invalidates the notion of a general intelligence factor and the claim that such a factor is responsible for the strategies an individual adopts or for the degree of transfer exhibited. It would appear that the human brain is not an " 'all purpose computer' . . . instead, there seems to be a multiplicity of systems for highly special tasks, e.g., the system for facial recognition appears to be separate from that for language. There is, at present, no good evidence . . . for the existence of a generalized logical deductive capacity" (2, p. 191).

When structural damage is present, often as not, new strategies are substituted for others. New "functional systems" take over, to use a term borrowed from Luria (3). For example, Dennis (cited in Geschwind) found that children who had undergone left decortication employed different strategies in certain linguistic tasks than did children with early right decortications whose strategies were more similar to those of normals (4, p. 190). Hence, the same task can be performed using variable neural structures and cognitive strategies.

Structural damage then may not automatically result in any lowering of general intellectual capacity but may rather, depending on the nature of the damage, destroy certain specialized capacities which vary in the extent to which they can be effectively replaced by new systems. Such a view is consistent with the complexity of behavioral symptoms which frequently accompany brain injury. For example, the patient may be unable to say the word "no" in response to a verbal command to do so, yet in response to a different command or request be able to respond, "No, I can't do that" (5, p. 122). Most probably, a different functional system was involved in the two instances.

Luria provides a striking example of the utility of a functional system. He describes the fact that often brain injured patients who could not take two successive steps when walking on a level floor were able to climb stairs without difficulty. Luria hypothesizes that in the flow of continuous movement involved in walking on a level floor, automatic processes take over controlled by involuntary systems located in the subcortical region, precisely that area injured in the individuals in question suffering from Parkinson's Disease. In climbing stairs, however, each step is an isolated movement which must be consciously organized, hence, higher cortical areas are implicated, areas which are still intact in these patients. Vygotsky was able to construct a laboratory model of the type of reorganization of movement involved in the two situations. He placed a series of papers on the floor asking patients to step over these. Under these circumstances, patients could now walk who previously could not take two steps in the room. Luria comments

We had helped the patient to overcome the symptoms of his dis-

24

ease by getting him to reorganize the mental processes he used in walking. He had compensated for his defect by transferring the activity . . . to the cortical level (6, p. 129).

The same principles are applicable to the intellectual domain. No wonder, then, that Luria found psychometric "measures of the intellect inadequate either to the task for which they had been designed or to the new applications" he desired to make (7, p. 133). Such psychometric measures assume that because an individual cannot perform the task *as presented* that the underlying requisite skills are absent. Clearly, this assumption is unwarranted. The task design may not be such so as to permit the manifestation of such skills. Further, it may be possible to train the individual to "reorganize his mental processes" so as to permit him to accomplish the task. Evidence that such training can be quite effective with the retarded, for example, and that it may be possible to train for transfer is discussed in a later chapter.

The brain injured individual may still possess intact a variety of preprogrammed specialized systems for learning. However, such programs may not be activated spontaneously as they are for an individual who has not suffered brain damage. Failure to transfer then may be due to difficulty in activating existing strategies and/or use of inappropriate strategies. A conceptualization in these terms, rather than in terms of general intellectual capacity, would suggest that so called general intellectual skills are potentially quite modifiable. It is hypothesized then that "there are elaborate preprogrammed systems of analysis, and action" and thought which can be modified or triggered by experience (8, p. 190).

Feuerstein's model of cognitive functioning and his assessment approach appears to be much more consistent than is Jensen's with the

25

neuropsychological literature concerning specialized systems in the brain and the possibilities for training of the brain damaged. He distinguishes between mental efficiency (or functional efficiency), a variable affected by parameters such as nature of the task, type, complexity, novelty, modality of presentation etcetera, and intellectual capacity. Psychometric measures provide information only as to functional efficiency rather than capacity. The tests are further "biased against individuals whose level of efficiency is low because of limited exposure or reduced automatization" (9, p.31). Research literature will be presented in Chapter Six demonstrating that functional efficiency can be markedly improved via, for instance, training for greater spontaneity and flexibility in the use of cognitive strategies.

Idiot Savants: A Challenge to Notions of General Intelligence

Idiot savant is a term used to describe mentally retarded individuals "demonstrating one or more skills above the level expected of non-retarded individuals" (10, p. 281). Such individuals are no doubt suffering from some type of neural damage, yet in certain areas these individuals possess remarkable competencies. For example, one case study reports on mentally retarded twins who were calendar calculators. One of the twins was presented with 302 dates randomly chosen between the years 100 and 40,406. The subject was to report the day of the week on which the dates occurred and answered 297 (97%) of these dates correctly (11).

Several savants have displayed remarkable skills in music, painting, mathematics, and other areas. One savant was able to give the square root of four digit numbers within an average of 4 seconds and to give the cube root of six digit numbers within 6 seconds (12).

Phenomenal memorization skills are frequently associated with other accompanying unusual skills of the savant. Another case involves a man who had memorized the population of every town in the United States in which the population was over 5000, the dates and basic information relating to over 2000 inventions and discoveries, the names, number of rooms and locations of 2000 hotels, statistics concerning 3000 mountains and rivers, and the county seat of every county in the United States (13).

Cases of savants include persons diagnosed as mentally retarded as the result of Down's syndrome, hydrocephalic, and microcephalic conditions as well as congenital syphilis. Hence, these persons are not always those who developed normally to a certain point and then suffered some brain trauma (14). At present, autopsies and other physiological investigations have not turned up specific features which characterize the savant and set him apart anatomically from other retarded individuals.

Several researchers (15, 16) have suggested that the savant may be quite capable of abstract thinking, at least as it relates to their specialized skill. This proposal has led to some controversy as it seems to create a contradiction in terms — a mentally retarded individual capable of that type of reasoning considered to be the hallmark of a superior intellect. Hill (17), for instance, contends it is more likely that the savant performs his prodigious feats via concrete means. This remains, however, a very open question and perhaps to a degree a moot one. It is relevant to note that the savant generally performs no better on tests of rote memory, such as digit span, than do other retarded individuals; suggesting that his specialized skills may not rely on such rote processes (18, p. 193).

To discount the savant's accomplishments because they may have been arrived at via cognitive strategies different from that which would typically be employed by a nonretarded individual would seem to constitute an arbitrary value judgement. At the root of the search to discover concrete reasoning underlying such unusual skills in the savant appears to be the hope of disqualifying such behaviors as a reflection of superior intelligence in a particular area.

The idiot savant serves to illustrate the weaknesses of the concept of general intelligence. One is led to agree with Beck that:

> One particularly unfortunate consequence of making general intelligence assessments and overlooking differences in types of intellectual abilities is that we lose sight of the fact that different people arrive at the same end via different intellectual means (19, p. 30).

Clearly, the general I.Q. test is not adequate to tap alternative approaches to problem solving, not only those employed by the savant but also the range of strategies used by the nonretarded individual.

Current psychometric measures of the intellect permit only that range of approaches suitable for dealing with the particular items on the test. An individual who scores poorly on an I.Q. test may yet be quite capable of displaying highly intelligent behavior, it is suggested, in a broader or narrower range of situations involving many of the skills I.Q. tests *purport* to measure. The assumption that psychometric measures serve to elicit a representative sample of the problem solving resources the individual has at his disposal is an unfounded one. The degree of conceptual understanding and the competencies the individual manifests on the test are in large part a function of the structural features of the assessment device. Failure to manifest a skill, then, cannot automatically be attributed to deficiencies inherent in the individual but may be due to deficiencies in the assessment measure (approach) itself.

Further complicating this issue is the fact that precisely what skills psychometric measures of the intellect call upon is unknown. For example, what cognitive process is it that the vocabulary test of the WISC and the Stanford-Binet taps? The answer is unclear as Estes notes:

> Considering how inextricably the vocabulary test has been bound up with the assessment of intelligence over nearly three-quarters of a century, it seems remarkable how little is known as to just what aspects of intellectual performance are being measured (20, p. 746).

Just as it is unclear what the test measures when assessing a successful performance, it is unclear which processing deficiencies are implicated when performance on a subtest is poor:

> Failure gives little diagnostic information, for it can come about in many qualitatively different ways. Inability to explain or define a word on request may occur because the necessary memory structure has never been established, because of a lack of retrieval cues for an intact memory structure, because words required to express the definition are at low availability owing to disuse, or because the individual lacks a general conception of the required solution to this type of problem and thus gives an answer which is meaningful within his own frame of reference but not within that of

the examiner (21, p. 747).

Jensen's Level I and Level II Abilities

Jensen labels as Level I abilities those involved in rote learning and short-term memory, and as Level II those implicated in tests of reasoning and problem solving: "Level I involves the registration and consolidation of stimulus inputs and the formation of simple association. There is little transformation of the input . . . Level II ability . . . involves self-initiated elaboration and transformation of the input . . ." (22, p. 549). Level II tests are held to have a much higher g loading and to represent a measure of information processing capacity. Further, Jensen claims blacks and whites differ much less on Level I tests (23, p. 549-50).

The neuropsychological literature previously discussed illustrates the weakness of such a conception. Problems can frequently be solved either via rote, automatic type processes or by more conscious, complex processing. Individuals given appropriate training and/or task arrangement are most often not confined to either type of problem solving approach. Hence, the brain injured subjects in Luria's study were able to substitute more deliberate conscious processing for the more automatic. Feuerstein has trained children of I.Q. 60-70 to "grasp, learn and then apply concepts requiring elaborations for transcending the simple circuit-type of associations characterizing Level I" (24, p. 78). He has trained retarded adolescents to solve Ravens Matrices which involve analogical reasoning skills, skills Jensen presumes would elude persons classified on the basis of I.Q. measures as confined to Level I modes of functioning.

Current psychometric measures are based upon an oversimplified neural model which postulates a preprogrammed general learning system rather than a great variety of systems specialized for the learning of various things. The model further advances the notion of a relatively static information processing capacity based upon neural efficiency. It, hence, ignores neuropsychological evidence for brain plasticity, including evidence of recovery from brain dysfunction resulting from therapeutic environments (25, 26).

In addition, rigid problem solving modes are attributed to the so-called lower I.Q. individual. Little or no allowance is provided for the possibility of training such individuals to adopt Level II reasoning skills. Their problem solving mode is held instead to be tied to certain relatively unmodifiable structural deficiencies in the brain (e.g., less neural complexity) which are thought to be genetically determined for the most part. The work of Feuerstein which clearly contradicts this latter tenet of the model is not examined in Jensen's text on "Bias in Mental Testing."

Research on training cognitive strategies in the mentally retarded and individuals classed as having learning difficulties is discussed in Chapter Six. The implications of such research for notions of intelligence as linked to genetically determined structural neural features is then considered.

On Brain Size, Neural Complexity and Intelligence

Jensen seems to have implicitly adopted the view of Thorndike (27) that persons who achieve higher scores on I.Q. tests possess brains which are structurally qualitatively different from persons who score

31

poorly. He (28) refers, for instance, to early work by Hooton, who attempts to relate occupational status to head circumference, the latter presumed to be related to brain size. Hooton claimed to have found that head circumferences of Boston whites in various occupational levels are in about the same rank order as is found when occupations are ranked according to average I.Q.'s. Hootan and Jensen fail to point out, however, that the sample sizes for the lowest and highest groups were widely discrepant as were the variances, making the results quite uninterpretable.

Relating variations in total size of the human brain with the intellect is a notion which dates back at least as far as the days of phrenology. Franz Hall (1758-1828) founded phrenology, a pseudo-science based on the premise that the brain was composed of several faculties and that development of any one of these resulted in an enlargement of the corresponding part of the brain and of the skull that covered it. It is important to note that autopsies have revealed that:

> plenty of . . . gifted men have had small brains and very ordinary men have had large ones. Although brain size has had a limited use in paleontology, we cannot by anatomical means be sure of telling the brain of a person with an I.Q. of 50 from that of a person with an I.Q. of 150 (29, p. 47).

Despite the absence of confirmatory evidence, the notion persists that variations in human intellect, within the normal range, are associated with variations in number of neural connections.

It is, of course, quite true that a class of retarded persons suffer from organic brain impairment which may involve abnormal brain size and neuronal loss (30). However, even in such instances it seems frequently not to be the case that poor intellectual performance is a function of structural defects in processing systems which are biologically based as is discussed in a later chapter. This issue appears to be much more complicated than the formula "faster, more complex brain equals brighter individual" would suggest.

REFERENCES

1. Jensen, A. R. *Bias in Mental Testing.* New York: The Free Press, 1980, p. 246.
2. Geschwind, N. Neurological knowledge and complex behaviors. *Cognitive Science,* 1980, 4, p. 185-193.
3. Luria, A. R. *The Making of Mind.* Cole, M. and Cole, S. (eds.), Cambridge: Harvard University Press, 1979.
4. Geschwind, Neurological knowledge, p. 190.
5. Luria, *The Making of Mind,* p. 122.
6. Ibid., p. 129.
7. Ibid., p. 133.
8. Geschwind, Neurological knowledge, p. 190.
9. Feuerstein, R., In collaboration with Rand, Y. and Hoffman, M. B. *The Dynamic Assessment of Retarded Performers.* Baltimore: University Park Press, 1979.
10. Hill, A. H. Savants: Mentally retarded individuals with special skills. In Ellis, N. R. (ed.), *International Review of Research in Mental Retardation.* New York: Academic Press, 1978.
11. Ibid., p. 278.
12. Ibid., p. 283.
13. Ibid., p. 283.
14. Ibid., p. 285.

15. Viscott, D. S. A musical idiot savant: A psychodynamic study, and some speculations on the creative process. *Psychiatry,* 1970, 33(4), p. 494-515.

16. Duckett, J. M. Idiot savants: Super specialization in mentally retarded persons. Unpublished doctoral dissertation, University of Texas at Austin, 1976.

17. Hill, Savants, p. 288.

18. Ibid., p. 293.

19. Beck, C. Why general intelligence assessment should be abandoned. *Interchange,* 1976-77, 7(3), p. 29-35.

20. Estes, W. K. Learning theory and intelligence. *American Psychologist,* October 1974, p. 740-749.

21. Ibid., p. 747.

22. Jensen, *Bias in Mental Testing,* p. 549.

23. Ibid., p. 549-550.

24. Feuerstein, *The Dynamic Assessment,* p. 78.

25. Luria, *The Making of Mind.*

26. Walsh, R. N. and Greenough, W. T. *Environments as Therapy for Brain Dysfunction.* New York: Plenum Press, 1976.

27. Thorndike, E. L. *Measurement of Intelligence.* New York: Teachers College, Columbia University, 1926.

28. Jensen, *Bias in Mental Testing,* p. 361

29. Oatley, R. *Brain Mechanisms and Mind.* London: Thames and Hudson, 1972, p. 47.

30. Isaacson, R. L. and Hartesveldt, C. V. The biological basis of an ethic for mental retardation. In Ellis, N. R. (ed.), *International Review of Research in Mental Retardation,* Volume 9, New York: Academic Press, 1978.

CHAPTER THREE

LOGICALLY FLAWED METAPHYSICAL ASSUMPTIONS UNDERLYING JENSEN'S POSITION

Measuring the Unknowable

This chapter discusses but a few of the more strikingly erroneous metaphysical assumptions Jensen makes; by no means is this list to be considered the definitive one.

Jensen may be justly characterized as a professed empiricist who, in reality, violates several of the fundamental tenets of positivism and empiricism in his work on intelligence. He advances the notion of "g", a mystical process, not manifest in any particular set of abilities or skills. "G" is held by Jensen to be the "hidden" mechanism underlying performance on the intelligence test. G, he further contends, cannot be identified with a delimited set of test items, its qualities supersede those processes which are allegedly tapped by specific test items. Jensen is anti-empiricist also in that he claims the existence of an abstract process — g — which has no specific referent in the physical world but is a property of "mind."

His emphasis upon intellectual measurement as useful, despite the fact that reasons for obtained differences in scores between populations are not in the least elucidated by the assessment, is an attempt to take a pragmatic stand. The pragmatist defines knowledge in terms of its utility. The weakness of this position is, of course, that there is no absolute standard of utility. With regards to mental measures, there is heated controversy as to their value, for they do not serve the interests of all populations in the culture equally well. The pragmatic approach to the definition of knowledge is reflected in Jensen's agreement with Miles who states that:

> The important point is not whether what we measure can appropriately be labelled "intelligence" but whether we have discovered something worth measuring. And this is not a matter that can be settled by an appeal to what is or is not the correct use of the word intelligent (1, p. 171).

Jensen, as Miles, implies that the argument between advocates of mental tests and opponents of current psychometric measures of the intellect is basically a semantic one. Yet, whether we have discovered something worth measuring is, contrary to Jensen's claims, a decision the scientist cannot make without conceptualizing what it is he is measuring. Does Jensen wish us to conclude that because test results are consistent with social stratification patterns for various populations, they are inherently worthwhile? Opponents would suggest that these tests are not worthwhile for precisely the same reason. The latter group would argue the tests are not measures of the intellect, but rather assess degree of cultural difference from the mainstream.

Jensen inadvertently rejects the acceptable scientific criterion for establishing the validity of particular knowledge claims — that of testability. That mental measures of the intellect assess "g" is not a directly testable hypothesis as it is unclear what g is or refers to. Jensen thus relies upon indirect evidence such as correlations between intelligence tests and other measures such as EVP (evoked visual potential) to argue that the former are measures of g. As is discussed in the next chapter such correlations do not provide evidence that mental tests assess basic intellect for the EVP, for example, is itself influenced by a number of psychological factors. Correlational data, in any case, are a weak basis for making assertions about the nature of the hypothetical g factor.

The general factor which emerges when diverse mental tests are intercorrelated is open to wide interpretation. It has been defined quite arbitrarily and with no convincing empirical support by Jensen and his supporters as a general intelligence factor. The factor could as well be conceptualized as a general acquired skill for dealing with personally irrelevant information presented out of context.

In asserting that tests measure something other than the task-specific skills the items tap, Jensen is abandoning also the position of the logical positivist who would hold that:

Intelligence is not an "occult" quality that "manifests" itself in test procedures: intelligence is precisely that which is studied by means of these procedures. The other definition tacitly assumes a non-scientific distinction between essence and appearance which is supposedly a manifestation of the essence. Science cannot operate meaningfully with statements that refer to some reality other than the qualities accessible to observation (2, p. 184).

It is Jensen rather than his opponents, then, who have conceptualized the notion of intelligence in such a way as to make it immeasurable in principle. Jensen puts the matter succinctly thus: "The g factor is not itself directly measurable" (3, p. 223-4). To take this position is to reject to a degree the empiricist approach, for the positivist will not admit of "invisible causes" that are "by definition inaccessible to human knowledge" (4, p. 4).

Jensen claims that differences assessed by mental tests are "real," in nature, and not artifacts of the measuring devices used (5, p. 737). What

Jensen does not acknowledge is that instruments or measuring devices, presuppose the validity of the principles which they embody, and are in fact an extension of theory. For instance, the I.Q. test embodies the notion that intelligence is normally distributed and is constructed so as to reify the principle. Jensen advances the circular argument that items were selected for the Binet and Wechsler scales without consciously intending to produce a normal distribution of I.Q. scores, yet a normal distribution was obtained *using the test as a measure of I.Q.* The point is, however, that features of the test — criteria for item selection — produce the normal curve, and there is no *independent* evidence for the normal distribution of I.Q.'s in nature (6, p. 71).

All measuring instruments are biased in the sense that they do not afford the means for independent tests of a theory, principle, or law. Additional examples include the thermometer which has built into it the principle that "bodies expand uniformly under the action of heat," yet we use thermometers to "ascertain the uniformity of thermic expansion. When we look at an object through a magnifying lens, we do not see the fringes of colored bands caused by diffraction and this is to presuppose the validity of certain laws of optics" (7, p. 131).

Differences between populations in assessed I.Q. scores are then a direct function of the nature of the measuring devices employed. The validity or reality, if you wish, of those differences are entirely dependent upon the validity of the principles embodied in the measuring device. The validity of these principles, as is discussed in the preceding and subsequent chapters, is highly suspect.

REFERENCES

1. Jensen, A. R. *Bias in Mental Testing.* New York: The Free Press, 1980.
2. Kolakowski, L. *The Alienation of Reason.* Garden City: Doubleday and Co., 1968.
3. Jensen, *Bias in Mental Testing,* p. 223-224.
4. Kolakowski, *The Alienation of Reason,* p. 4.
5. Jensen, *Bias in Mental Testing,* p. 737.
6. Ibid., p. 71.
7. Kolakowski, *The Alienation of Reason,* p. 131.

PART II

WHAT MENTAL TESTS MEASURE

CHAPTER FOUR

DO MENTAL TESTS MEASURE
BASIC COGNITIVE PROCESSES?

One of Jensen's major points is his claim that mental measures assess basic cognitive processes identified with the "g" factor and not simply acquired skills and cognitive strategies. Related to this assumption is his assertion that black-white racial differences on mental tests are a function of the test's g loading, with differences increasing for tests which are more highly g loaded. Less culture-loaded tests, he asserts, are better measures of g and hence accentuate the black-white differential in performance on mental tests (1, p. 585).

Jensen does not provide convincing evidence to suggest that mental measures assess something apart from acquired cognitive skills. He refers instead to studies of correlations between such measures as reaction time, evoked potential and I.Q. He assumes that RT and evoked potential are relatively pure measures of neural efficiency uncontaminated by factors such as motivation and knowledge, and that therefore the correlation of these measures with I.Q. is evidence for the fact that mental measures tap basic cognitive processes and not simply acquired skills.

The greater black-white differential on culture-reduced, highly g loaded tests he also takes as evidence that mental measures assess differences in fundamental aspects of cognitive process rather than experiential factors.

In addition, he attributes the correlation in the .70's of summed scores on Piagetian type tasks with Binet scores to the fact that both are measures of g — of cognitive capacity and mental maturation — as opposed to learned strategies.

The inadequacy of such evidence as that mentioned by Jensen to substantiate the claim that mental measures assess other than acquired skills is examined in the next section.

RT and its Correlation with g

Jensen unabashedly asserts:

If we have learned nothing else of fundamental importance from these reaction time studies as yet, they have surely proved beyond a reasonable doubt that the g of standard psychometric tests of mental ability reflects individual differences in cognitive processes that are far more general and far more profound than anything suggested by the popular notion of I.Q. tests as reflecting only differences in cognitive contents and skills that persons have chanced to learn in school or acquire in a cultured home (2, p. 704).

G, according to Jensen, has to do with capacity for information processing and RT studies he assumes are unconfounded measures of the same. Correlations between the two, then, take on special significance in view of his assumptions regarding RT measures.

There are a great variety of RT measures and variations in RT studies; but a few will be examined here with a view to pointing out some general problems which are common to most and bear upon Jensen's assumptions.

Hunt's RT Studies

Jensen cites Hunt's finding that RTs on a task involving same-different judgements correlate with scores on the verbal part of the Scholastic Aptitude Test (3). In this task, subjects are presented with letters that are either physically the same (e.g., AA) or physically different (e.g., AB) or physically different but with the same name (e.g., Aa). Subjects are to press one of two buttons labelled "same" or "different" — "same" referring to pairs of letters with the same name. University students take about 75 milliseconds longer to respond to same name-physically different pairs (e.g., Aa), than to same name-physically identical pairs (e.g., AA). Subjects scoring in the upper quartile of the SAT-verbal subtest require less time to make these RT decisions, with the effect more marked for same name-physically different pairs.

The argument Jensen is making on the basis of Hunt's data is that high verbal subjects retrieve information from long-term memory more quickly than do low verbal subjects. In order to make the same-different (name) judgement for "Aa" pairs, it is assumed subjects must contact long-term memory stores for the name, while "AA" or "aa" pairs can be identified as same name without such memory processing simply on the basis of identity of physical features. The RTs are taken to be pure measures of information processing skills uninfluenced by experiential factors.

Kolers points out, however, that subjects are more experienced in identifying similarity on the basis of physical similarity rather than linguistic features. "We are far more likely to note that two papers, two pictures, or two letters 'look alike' than we are in noting that they have the same name . . . " (4, p. 196). Hence, Kolers highlights the fact that such a task is very much influenced by prior skills. Contrary to Jensen's claims, Kolers also points out that in such studies there is typically as large a variation between items falling into one class as another. Hence,

45

in one study RTs to physically different — different name pairs all to be classified according to physical identity—ranged from 395 to 547 milliseconds. The difference of 75 milliseconds between AA and Aa pairs judged on the basis of same or different name then loses much of its apparent significance. It would seem that making judgements of sameness on the basis of physical identity alone is also a highly complex and abstract business. Kolers notes in light of such difficulties that, "Here we have an example of the conceptual dangers, in the absence of a supportive theory, of using differences in time as an index of differences in processing . . . " (5, p. 199). It is important to note that "no theory predicts that the different judgements (e.g., same name vs. physically same) should vary in time; rather, the differences in time are used to create a theory" (6, p. 175). It is not at all clear, then, what such RT differences signify.

Jensen's assertion that the "RT experiment refutes the notion that individual differences in g are largely the result of individual differences in learned strategies" (7, p. 700) is overstating the case, to say the least. Typical RTs in such studies are considerably longer than the time needed (160 milliseconds) to relay simple information such as a flash to the visual cortex. Many operations, Kolers points out, can have taken place on the input during intervals of from 300-600 milliseconds. These operations may be importantly influenced by learning in ways which are not yet understood. It seems quite feasible then that RTs are long enough to allow for a strategy explanation of individual differences in such tasks. Jensen's assumption that RTs in his light-button experiment are too short to allow for the influence of cognitive strategies may also be premature. It is a claim reminiscent of earlier psychologists' distinctions between perception and sensation, based on time parameters.

Keele (8) presents evidence that RT depends partly upon S-R compatibility and practice. For instance, a study by Mowbray and Rhoades (9) demonstrated that extensive practice in an RT task involving key presses to lights resulted in performance in a four choice situation equalling that of the two choice situation. RT results are then not simply a function of informational complexity of the task; factors such as practice do generally make a difference.

Hick's law — the finding that RT or decision time increases as a linear function of the number of "bits" of information to be processed — it is here contended, will not be a major contribution "to discovering the nature of g" (10, p. 672) contrary to Jensen's claim. The law does *not* predict decision time for a particular amount of information. Such is not the case in that the constant "b" in the Hick-Hyman law ($RT = bHt$) varies according to relationships between stimulus and response and with differing amounts of practice. RT measures then assess experience with the specifics of a task as much as they do any presumed basic information processing capacity. If Jensen has concluded learning does not play a significant role in many RT tasks, it is here suggested that his designs have not been set up to manifest such effects.

It is not at all clear further just what aspect of processing RT measures are tapping. "Some models assume that the primary determinant of RT is the time necessary to identify a stimulus rather than the time necessary to retrieve information regarding appropriate responses" (11, p. 35). For instance, in a study by Posner and Mitchell, it was found that subjects were able to judge unfamiliar nonsense forms as physically identical as fast as they could do so for letters with which they had years of experience (12). In such a case RT does not seem to be reflecting

47

aspects of memory retrieval but rather something concerning initial precategorical sensory encoding.

Since it is not clear what it is differences in RT signify with regard to information processing, correlations between RT and mental measures can hardly be held to validate claims that mental measures assess something profound about cognitive process. While one is led to agree with Jensen that "measurement and theory develop hand and hand" (13, p. 173), it appears to be the case in the field of psychometrics that instead measurement has been substituted for adequate conceptual models of the nature of intelligence.

Hunt takes his research on RT to suggest that "intelligence really means something" (14, p. 323). He assumes that "present performance including performance on an intelligence test, is an amalgamation of knowledge and information processing capacity" (15, p. 321). The question of utmost importance is the relationship between information processing capacity and learned cognitive strategies. Can these be distinguished conceptually in any meaningful sense? What do findings that scanning rates of short-term memory are related to verbal intelligence signify?

Love and Hunt (16) report the case of a mnemonist whose scanning rate was twice as fast as that reported for college students using comparable material. Clearly, then, strategies can have a tremendous impact upon information processing capacity. Individuals with encephalitic infection and thus probable brain damage were found to have unusually high scan rates in a study by Harris and Fleer (17). To what degree then can the training of strategies enhance cognitive capacity? Are there structural limitations to the improvements in intellectual functioning which can be achieved, as Hunt assumes there are?

These questions are addressed in Chapter 6.

Evoked Potentials and g States

Jensen states that brain electrical potentials are not cognitive processes at all and hence that their measurement is extremely culture-
reduced (18, p. 708). There is a long history of attempts to relate evoked
potentials to I.Q. on the assumption that high I.Q. individuals ought to
show shorter latencies of neural electrical discharge in response to
stimulation. Jensen himself concedes that "the AEP and I.Q. research
picture soon becomes a thicket of seemingly inconsistent and confus-
ing findings, confounded variables, methodological differences,
statistically questionable conclusions, unbridled theoretical specula-
tion . . . " (19, p. 709). Nevertheless, the search for the organic basis of
g continues. The correlation between critical flicker fusion and I.Q. has
also been investigated but Jensen admits that results "overall look
unimpressive" (20, p. 707). Despite such disclaimers, Jensen flatly
asserts later in his text that correlations of measures such as flicker
fusion threshold and EEG recordings of average latency and amplitude
of brain potential with I.Q. scores suggest that I.Q. measures something
more basic than but acquired skill (21, p. 714).

Jensen's claim that evoked potentials are rather pure measures of
neural efficiency, unaffected by cognitive variables and social influences, is inconsistent with a body of neurological evidence pointing to
the modifiability of ECP (evoked cortical potential) via a number of
cognitive variables; e.g., Sutton *et al.* (22, 23).

Commenting on this literature Shipley states:

The many reports in the literature of the influence on the evoked cortical potential of attention, information, expectancy and cognitive processes in general are convincing evidence of psychological factors in the electrogenesis of these late brain responses . . . the key problem in this work is the difficulty of distinguishing response components which are . . . invariant . . . from those components which are readily malleable under cognitive and psychological pressures (24, p. 120).

The features of evoked cortical potential, then, would appear to reflect in large part the results of training, the peculiarities of task design and how such factors influence the individual's attentional processes, for instance.

Correlations between I.Q. and aspects of the EVP are as yet unimpressive, but in any case it would seem that such correlations are not to be taken as evidence for the view that intelligence tests measure something akin to "pure" information processing capacity, uncontaminated by experiential factors. Training has been found to modify features of the evoked potential in Downs Syndrome children, for example (25). Callaway reviews several lines of evidence suggesting that evoked potentials reflect cognitive responses and not some basic neurophysiological processes underlying intelligence. For instance, amount of reduction in amplitude and shortening of latency in visual potentials over the course of a perceptual experiment appears to be related to the fact that bright persons become bored easily as the findings were correlated with reports of boredom. Callaway concludes "The results may depend not so much on neural efficiency as upon the fact that bright subjects are easier to bore than dull subjects" (26, p. 555).

In the next section are examined attempts to imbue intelligence tests with construct validity via linking them to Piagetian tasks — the claim being that both assess cognitive maturation.

Piagetian Tasks as Measures of g

Jensen suggests that Piagetian tasks are culture-reduced, highly g loaded measures. He notes that "white-black differences on Piaget's tasks are of about the same magnitude as on such conventional standardized I.Q. tests as the Stanford-Binet and Wechsler" (27, p. 713). The great variability of correlations between Piagetian tasks and conventional measures of the intellect Jensen explains away as due to flaws in the experimental design of studies investigating such correlations (28, p. 673).

In this section is examined the question of whether the correlation between Piagetian tasks and conventional intelligence measures signifies that psychometric measures assess basic cognitive process, that is information processing capacity apart from acquired skills. In order to consider this issue, it is of course necessary to clarify first what it is Piagetian tasks assess. Jensen asserts that what Piagetian tasks assess at any stage is "not items of acquired *knowledge*, . . . but unconscious cognitive structures or schemas that develop through the child's interaction with those most common aspects of the environment that are universally available to virtually *all* biologically normal children" (29, p. 670).

Piagetian tasks have been criticized as being as much measures of linguistic as of cognitive capacities and deficiencies (30). For instance, the tasks used to assess preoperational skills often require the child to comprehend relational terms such as "more" and "less." There is considerable evidence that young children in the age group considered to correspond to the stage of preoperational thinking have great difficulty with such relational terms (31, 32). Furthermore, linguistic competence with regard to the use of relational terms is correlated with problem solving skills on Piagetian tasks. Hence, conservers (children who recognize, for example, that the quantity of liquid remains unchanged if it is poured from a tall vessel into a short wide vessel) use terms such as "more-less," "tall and short" more adequately than do nonconservers (33, 34). The structure of the questions asked children in such tasks has also been found to influence whether a correct response is given (35). Siegel points out, in view of such evidence that "observed differences in cognitive functioning (on Piagetian tasks) may be a reflection of the differences in language ability" (36, p. 45).

Language skills, of course, are open to considerable modification and variation as the result of learning experiences. Siegel has designed a number of nonverbal tasks analagous to more traditional Piagetian tasks which seem to challenge many assumptions regarding age related logical abilities. For instance, one series of studies (37) demonstrates that four and five year olds often can conserve number contrary to Piagetian claims. Children of this age were found to be capable of matching a sample array of dots to one of four alternative arrays based upon numerical equivalence. The set size of the sample and the alternatives varied randomly on every trial. These same children were often unable to solve traditional Piagetian conservation of number tasks. Such findings lead Siegel to conclude that, "Assessment with the Piagetian tasks appears to be producing many 'false negatives.' Systematic biases in the Piagetian tasks prevent the child's logical abilities from emerging" (38, p. 61). Given these difficulties with

Piagetian tasks it seems inappropriate to suggest, as Jensen does, that small correlations of standard psychometric measures with such tasks attest to the fact that both measure basic cognitive capacity.

It would seem that Piagetian tasks can no more directly assess basic information processing capacity than do standardized psychometric measures. What abilities are attributed to the individual are always in large part a function of the task itself and how that ability is conceptualized by the designer of the task. Nevertheless, the debate goes on with various parties taking opposing stands on whether Piagetian tasks are interchangeable with psychometric measures of intelligence or whether they assess something quite different than a general intelligence factor (39, 40, 41).

Evidence discussed in the preceding chapter suggests that current mental tests are assessing learned skills in combination with any hypothetical basic information processing capacity. The psychometric approach to the assessment of the intellect involves measuring the ability to utilize a restricted set of skills and retrieve a narrow range of information. More comprehensive, process-oriented approaches are examined in chapter 11.

REFERENCES

1. Jensen, A. R. *Bias in Mental Testing.* New York: The Free Press, 1980, p. 585.
2. Ibid., p. 704.
3. Hunt, E. Varieties of cognitive power. In L. B. Resnick (ed.), *The*

Nature of Intelligence, p. 237-259. Hillsdale, N. J.: Erlbaum, 1976.

4. Kolers, P. Some problems of classification, In Kavanagh, J. F. and Mattingly, J. G. (eds.) *Language by Ear and by Eye.* Cambridge: MIT Press, 1972, p. 196.

5. Ibid., p. 199.

6. Ibid., p. 195.

7. Jensen, *Bias in Mental Testing,* p. 700.

8. Keele, S. W. *Attention and Human Performance. Pacific Palisades: Goodyear Publishing Company Inc., 1973.*

9. Mowbray, G. H. and Rhoades, M. U. On the reduction of choice-reaction time with practice. *Quarterly Journal of Experimental Psychology,* 1959, 11, p. 16-23.

10. Jensen, *Bias in Mental Testing,* p. 692.

11. Keele, *Attention and Human Performance,* p. 85.

12. Posner, M. I. and Mitchell, R. A chronometric analysis of classification. *Psychological Review,* 1967, 74, p. 392-409.

13. Jensen, *Bias in Mental Testing,* p. 173.

14. Hunt, E. We know who knows, but why? In Anderson, R. C., Spiro, R. J. and Montague, W. E. (eds.) *Schooling and the Acquisition of Knowledge.* New York: John Wiley and Sons, 1977.

15. Ibid., p. 321.

16. Love, T., and Hunt, E. Information processing characteristics of very good memorizers. Technical Report, Department of Psychology, University of Washington, October, 1975.

17. Harris, G. J. and Fleer, R. E. High speed memory scanning in mental retardates: Evidence for a central processing deficit. *Journal of Experimental Child Psychology,* 1974, 17, p. 452-459.

18. Jensen, *Bias in Mental Testing,* p. 708.

19. Ibid., p. 709.

20. Ibid., p. 707.

21. Ibid., p. 714.

22. Sutton, S. Braren, M. and Zubin, J. Evoked potential correlates of stimulus uncertainty. *Science,* 1965, 150, p. 1187-1188.

23. Sutton, S., Braren, M., Zubin, J. and John, E. R. Information delivery and the sensory evoked potential. *Science,* 1967, 155, p. 1436-1439.

24. Shipley, T. *Sensory Integration in Children: Evoked Potentials and Intersensory Functions in Pediatrics and Psychology.* Springfield: Charles C. Thomas Publishing, 1980.

25. Marcus, M. M. and Schafer, E. W. P. Evoked response as a measure of development. Presented at the symposium on Innovations in the Electrophysiological and Behavioral Assessment of Mental Retardation, 53rd Annual Convention of the Western Psychological Association, April 1973, Annaheim, California.

26. Callaway, E. Correlations between average evoked potentials and measures of intelligence. *Archives of General Psychiatry,* 1974, 29, p. 553-558.

27. Jensen, *Bias in Mental Testing,* p. 713.

28. Ibid., p. 673.

29. Ibid., p. 670.

30. Siegel, L. S. The relationship of language and thought in the preoperational child: A reconsideration of nonverbal alternatives to Piagetian tasks. In Siegel, L. S. and Brainerd, C. J. (eds.), *Alternatives to Piaget: Critical Essays on the Theory.* New York: Academic Press, 1978.

31. Donaldson, M. and Wales, R. J. On the acquisition of some rela-

tional terms. In Hayes, J. R. (ed.), *Cognition and the Development of Language.* New York: Wiley, 1970.

32. Donaldson, M. and Balfour, G. Less is more: A study of language comprehension in children. *British Journal of Psychology,* 1968, 59, p. 461-471.

33. Sinclair-de-Zwart, H. Developmental psycholinguistics. In Elkind, D. and Flavell, J. H. (eds.), *Studies in Cognitive Development.* New York: Oxford University Press, 1969.

34. Bruner, J. S. and Kennedy, H. J. On multiple ordering. In Bruner, J. S. *et al* (eds.), *Studies in Cognitive Growth.* New York: Wiley, 1966.

35. Goodnow, J. J. Compensation arguments on conservation tasks. *Developmental Psychology,* 1973, 8, p. 140.

36. Siegel, The relationship of language and thought, p. 45.

37. Siegel, L. S. The role of spatial arrangement and heterogeneity in the development of concepts of numerical equivalence. *Canadian Journal of Psychology,* 1973, 27, p. 351-355.

38. Ibid., p. 61.

39. Glass, G. V. and Stephens, J. Reply to Humphreys' and Parsons' "Piagetian tasks measure intelligence and intelligence tests measure cognitive development." *Intelligence,* 1980, 4, p. 171-174.

40. Kohlberg, L. and DeVries, R. Don't throw out the Piagetian baby with the psychometric bath: reply to Humphreys and Parsons. *Intelligence,* 1980, 4, p. 175-177.

41. Humphreys, L. G. Methinks they do protest too much. *Intelligence,* 1980, 4, p. 179-183.

CHAPTER FIVE

CONTEMPORARY COGNITIVE AND NEUROPSYCHOLOGICAL RESEARCH:
IMPLICATIONS FOR THE MEASURE OF THE INTELLECT

Introduction

What is suggested in this section is that measurement of basic intellectual competence isolated from the products of a particular learning history is an unattainable objective. What is possible is assessment of particular acquired problem solving modes. It is as nonfeasible to attempt to disentangle intellectual skill from the teaching or experiential context as it is to attempt to assess the value of an instructional approach in the abstract, without considering its impact on the students with whom it is to be employed. Yet Jensen and his supporters advance the view that intelligence is directly measurable apart from a consideration of experiential factors or quality of education.

On the Acquisition of Knowledge

Brown comments, " . . . much of what we regard as intelligent thinking is an outcome of a specialized set of educational experiences which are discontinuous from those encountered in everyday life, experiences which promote different modes of learning and knowing" (1, p. 251). It is here argued that it is precisely these specialized sets of educational experiences which current measures of the intellect are designed to assess, and that they are as a result measuring acquired skills in precisely the same fashion as do achievement tests. Jensen himself concedes that, "No clear-cut *operational* distinction can be made between aptitude (intelligence) tests and achievement tests" (2, p. 239). It is here also argued that no reasonable logical distinction between the two is possible.

The focus in this chapter is then upon the effects of schooling on cognition (intelligent behavior). This because most measures of the intellect are designed, it is here held, to assess skills acquired via schooling.

Luria's Research on Cultural Differences in Thinking

Contemporary cognitive and neuropsychological research clearly demonstrates the difficulties in distinguishing between culturally based differences in thinking, and differences originating from the quantum of "g" (general intelligence) the individual is allegedly in possession of. The literature reveals that experiential factors determine in large part not only what the individual knows but how he knows (thinks). Simply attempting to control for familiarity of materials presented, and verbal requirements, as is the case with allegedly culture-reduced tests, is thus quite inadequate to assure that mental measures assess intellect rather than cultural difference.

Luria (3) was one of the first to examine cultural differences in thought processes as the result of differential exposure to schooling. Luria studied women and peasants in remote villages who were illiterate, women who had no formal schooling but had attended short-term courses in the teaching of kindergartens, collective farm workers who had taken short courses and held some sort of office but were barely literate, and finally women who had attended school for two to three years and planned to become teachers eventually. Luria's intention was to examine shifts in "the basic forms, as well as in the content of people's thinking" (4, p. 60) as a function of variations in cultural experience.

He found significant differences in the problem solving approach on diverse tasks, both verbal and non-verbal, as a function of cultural experience. In naming and categorizing a set of geometric figures, for instance, illiterates tended to rely on names of concrete objects and also to classify based upon association with such objects, rather than abstracted perceptual similarities between the figures. In categorizing concrete objects, groupings reflected what Luria terms "situational" thinking (5, p. 69). Objects were grouped according to their relevance in a particular situation rather than any common attribute. For example, one peasant grouped pictures of a hammer, saw, log, and hatchet together on the basis that they are all needed if one wishes to saw and split a log. Another grouped pictures of two adults and a child together explaining that the boy would be used to run errands while the adults could continue with the work at hand. These findings then reveal that the exigencies of practical life dominated the thought forms of the illiterate.

Persons who had but attended a year or two of schooling relied much more than did the unschooled upon categorical classification based on abstracted attributes. For instance, the schooled individual responded as to which three objects can be grouped together of the following: a glass, pan, spectacles, and a bottle — that the glass, spectacles and bottle go together as they are all glass while the pan must be set apart as it is metal (6, p. 71). Similar effects were obtained in syllogistic reasoning tasks. Luria concludes from his work:

> Changes in the practical forms of activity, and especially the reor-
> ganization of activity based on formal schooling, produced qual-
> itative changes in the thought processes of the individuals studied
> . . . basic changes in the organization of thinking can occur in a
> relatively short period when there are sufficiently sharp changes in
> socio-historical circumstances (7, p. 80).

The work of Luria demonstrates the profound effects of even relatively short schooling experiences. Current mental measures provide
little or no insights into how such factors have contributed to the test
performance.

Not only does schooling appear to facilitate theoretical (abstract)
versus practically-oriented thought forms, but it also encourages the
application of general principles to classes of problems. Unschooled
populations have particular difficulties in transferring acquired skills
from one set of problems or tasks to a related set (8). It is inappropriate
to infer, then, as does Jensen, that difficulties in transfer necessarily
reflect the limitations of the intollect. These constraints on the application of knowledge can just as well reveal inadequacies in cultural or
experiential preparation for the same.

Current mental measures may present problems the solutions to
which call for "schooled" logic rather than any "natural" logic.
The unschooled have difficulty evaluating syllogisms which refer to
facts of which they have no direct knowledge, e.g., given the syllogism
"All Kpelle men are rice farmers. Mr. Smith is not a rice farmer. Is he a
Kpelle man?" unschooled persons refuse to consider the problem if
they don't know Mr. Smith (9). So, too, the individual who does poorly
on a psychometric test of intelligence may be most often unprepared to
deal with the specialized types of logic the test demands. That lack of

preparation being not a reflection of deficient intellect but of a lack of prerequisite training and acquired skills relevant to these specific task demands. Just as we erroneously tend to regard the illiterate as lacking in intelligence because his thinking style may differ from ours, so too the individual who does not respond appropriately to the narrow range of problem types presented on a test of "intelligence" is too often automatically regarded as mentally incompetent to some degree.

In both cases, the fundamental error is the assumption that skills in dealing with the problems of interest reflect the level of mental or cognitive development attained. However, "far from being the natural outcome of maturation (these skills) are very much dependent on the intervention of (and quality of) formal schooling" (10, p. 249). Jensen is quite misleading, it would seem, in arguing simultaneously that psychometric measures of the intellect assess something more fundamental than simply acquired skills, and also that test users and developers can remain agnostic on the question of the factors determining differences in mean scores on intelligence tests across, for instance, black versus white populations. Clearly, Jensen has, without adequate empirical support, ruled out cultural difference explanations while at the same time claiming neutrality on the issue of the genesis of differences in test performance. The two positions are, of course, contradictory.

Recent Cross-Cultural Studies on Intellectual Process

Goodnow presents cross-cultural evidence that raises important questions about "the way we define intelligent behavior and the way we measure it" (11, p. 169). She points out, for instance, that relations

61

among different tasks often do not remain consistent across various cultural groups. Thus tasks which are "thought to belong together because they are, in our culture, statistically tied to one another, or on theoretical grounds, regarded as tapping the same abilities" are often found not to "go together" in other cultures (12, p. 170). For example, while Western schooled children in one study tended to acquire conservation of volume concepts and combinatorial reasoning at about the same time, Chinese boys with little or no schooling did well on the conservation task, but very poorly on the combinatorial reasoning task. Similar inconsistencies are also found for different forms of the same task (13, 14).

Cross-cultural data reveal that controlling for familiarity of the task is a complex matter which has been but crudely analyzed. Goodnow (15, p. 172) explains that "Familiarity may refer to the material itself (e.g. shapes), to an operation (e.g. grouping or counting), or to an operation applied to particular material (e.g. grouping or counting shapes)". So-called culture-free and culture-fair tests are rarely, if ever, scrutinized as to whether they are or are not familiar to the subject in all of the respects mentioned above. In the absence of such a detailed analysis, Jensen's claim that current mental measures are immune to cultural differences is open to contention.

The suggestion has been made that many skills in Non-Western cultures may be more context-bound or less generalizable than in Western cultures. "G" may thus be the byproduct of a particular sort of cultural training rather than a manifestation of native general intelligence. Generalization to new contexts may not be a culturally valued or reinforced skill among certain peoples. Alternatively, Goodnow suggests, behavior:

may be no more specific in other cultures than it is in our own, but rather the threads that bind situations or performances together may not be the same as in our culture and may not be represented in the tasks we assemble. They may in fact not be known to us (16, p. 172).

Such considerations pertaining to cross-cultural data are pertinent also to an evaluation of the adequacy of mental tests as applied to diverse groups within cultures. Such data highlight the fact that non-display of a particular set of skills or behaviors on a mental test need not indicate an inherent cognitive deficiency as is implied by the notion of a general intelligence measure. Rather, failure to display certain of the requisite behaviors or skills may be due to any one of several factors such as the fact that: "The information needed for the task has not been needed before, or it has been needed but remains tied to some other context" (17, p. 176). The implication is then that there is "a need for new learning — learning that supplies new information, demonstrates a new extension of what is known, or overcomes resistance to an altered way of looking at a problem" (18, p. 176). Unfortunately, mental tests, aptitude tests, tests of learning disabilities and so on, are rather weak in pinpointing those areas where new learning or relearning is needed (19, 20). This because the tests provide little insight into the dynamics of the cognitive process which underlies the poor performance. In addition, many of the tests such as the S.A.T., for instance, are used exclusively for selection purposes, not as a means to assist individuals to acquire whatever skills they may be lacking.

This author is in full accord with Goodnow that "a great deal remains to be learned about assumptions dealing with proper methods, good answers, and reasonable tasks" (21, p. 185). Jensen, in contrast, contends that most, if not all, of the tasks that comprise the better known mental tests such as the WISC, and S.A.T. are "reasonable", and quite accurate measures of cognitive competencies. The cross-cultural data and the issues arising therefrom provide yet another indicator that Jensen has presented an unduly favorable evaluation of the adequacy of such assessment devices.

Olson's Research on the Literate Bias of Schooling: Implications for Assessing the Intellect

Olson explains that "schooling involves the acquisition of knowledge that possesses at least two distinctive properties: (1) that knowledge is divorced from practical action, and (2) that knowledge is represented in terms of linguistic symbols" (22, p. 65). We have come to the fallacious popular conclusion that acquisition of this very specialized form of knowledge is a clear demonstration of adequate intellect. Hence, intelligence test results are often correlated with school achievement in order to provide evidence for predictive validity.

Olson's work demonstrates that "knowledge is activity and context specific" (23, p. 69). School achievement is thus a particularly inadequate criterion to employ in predictive validity studies of psychometric measures of the intellect because such achievement reflects very specialized acquired skills and knowledge, rather than general intelligence. Any correlations that do exist between school achievement and I.Q. scores would then imply that the intelligence test itself most probably also assesses such acquired context specific skills, rather than basic general intellectual competence. An example of such specialized skills required for both good performance at school and on an I.Q. test will illustrate the point. In school, as on an intelligence test, the student must often respond to the logical form of the problem or questions posed and not according to imposed personal meanings. To view such a skill as a reflection of intellect is unfounded for the skill appears to be a direct function of extent of formal schooling the individual has received and his degree of literacy. Olson and his colleagues (24) found, for instance, that five year olds' ability to recognize the logical implications of oral statements was determined by their knowledge of the characters mentioned in the statement. For instance, if presented with the sentence "John was hit by Mary. Did Mary hit John?" ability to answer the question correctly depended on whether the child knew who Mary and John were. Schooling provides children experience with tasks which demand the suppression of such idiosyncratic attributions of meaning and culture-specific responses. Acquisition of this skill represents not cognitive maturation, nor intellectual development, but rather the effects of formal schooling.

It will be recalled that in the discussion of Luria's work with adult illiterates that these individuals, as the young child in Olson's study not exposed to schooling, responded to verbal tasks (syllogisms) in terms of personal prior knowledge and not appreciation of the logical form of the syllogism.

Schooling appears to profoundly affect performance on a range of verbal and nonverbal tasks via a number of different mechanisms such as memory (alluded to in Chapter 1) and thinking style discussed in this chapter. There is simply not sufficient empirical evidence to suggest that so-called psychometric measures of the intellect are uncontaminated by such factors, that they measure exclusively something other than the effects of differences in the quality of education.

Knowledge Acquisition as a Function of Intellect
Versus Instructional Mode

Olson's research reveals that what is learned depends in part upon mode of instruction. Hence, mental measures which allegedly assess differences in acquisition of (knowledge) content and ability to apply that knowledge are, in fact, also assessing differences in instructional mode. For example, Olson (25) found that ability to transfer information is a function of instructional mode. Students who learned proverbs using paraphrases (either provided or self-generated) showed more transfer to new proverbs than subjects who learned the original set via rehearsal. It would seem the groups understood the proverbs in different ways or at different levels as a function of varying modes of instruction. Grover (26) also found that mode of instruction and media influenced level of conceptual understanding on a transfer task. Children trained to duplicate three-dimensional block designs in a situation which called for inference, transferred their knowledge of the designs to the identical patterns in two-dimensions more adequately than did children originally trained simply to copy the designs under optimal cue conditions. It can be assumed then that the "inference group" acquired both differing skills and knowledge of the designs as a function of the specifics of the instructional mode used.

Other studies of Olson's demonstrate that knowledge is dependent upon the medium of instruction such that a concept such as "diagonality" can sometimes be understood in one medium and not another (27). Knowledge (content) and skills acquired are not independent of instructional mode nor of the tasks used to demonstrate the same. It is fundamentally incorrect then to assume, as does Jensen, "the indifference of the indicator." Both the particularities of item (task) format and instructional mode determine ability to gain and/or apply knowledge. Poor performance on an intelligence test is thus dependent upon whether the individual has been exposed to those instructional modes likely to instill the relevant task-specific skills. The fact that the black-white gap in school achievement *increases* with length of schooling (28) suggests that instructional modes employed with minority group students are inadequate. The inadequacies of such schooling are manifest on psychometric measures. At the same time, it seems to be quite possible to instill in these groups via training the necessary task-specific skills for adequate performance on both verbal and nonverbal alleged measures of the intellect (29). It is, given empirical evidence for the context-specific nature of knowledge, particularly disheartening to read Jensen's suggestion that some groups be exposed only to instructional methodologies which focus upon rote, lower level cognitive skills, even if the methods themselves are not rote (30, 31). It would seem that certain children's (e.g. black Americans) lower performance on psychometric tests of achievement and intellect is, in fact, the result of just such an emphasis in the education of minority group children which exists at present.

REFERENCES

1. Brown, A. L. Development, Schooling and the Acquisition of Knowledge About Knowledge. In Anderson, R. C., Spiro, R. J. and Montague, W. E. (eds.), *Schooling and the Acquisition of Knowledge.* New York: John Wiley and Sons, 1977, p. 241-254.

2. Jensen, A. R. *Bias in Mental Testing.* New York: The Free Press, 1980, p. 239.

3. Luria, A. R. *Cognitive Development: The Cultural and Social Foundations.* Cambridge: Harvard University Press, 1976.

4. Luria, A. R. *The Making of Mind: A Personal Account of Soviet Psychology.* Cole, M. and Cole, S. (eds.), Cambridge: Harvard University Press, 1979.

5. Ibid., p. 69.

6. Ibid., p. 71.

7. Ibid., p. 80.

8. Scribner, S. and Cole, M. Cognitive consequences of formal and informal education. *Science,* 1973, 182, p. 553-559.

9. Brown, Development, Schooling and the Acquisition of Knowledge about Knowledge, p. 249.

10. Ibid.

11. Goodnow, J. J. The Nature of Intelligent Behavior: Questions Raised by Cross-Cultural Studies. In Resnick, L. B. (ed.), *The Nature of Intelligence.* New York: John Wiley and Sons, 1976, p. 169-187.

12. Ibid., p. 170.

13. Glick, J. Cognitive Development in Cross-Cultural Perspective. In Horowitz, F. D. (ed.), *Review of Child Development Research,* Vol. 4, Chicago: University of Chicago Press, 1975.

14. Cole, M., Gay, J., and Glick, J. Some experimental studies of Kpelle quantitative behavior. *Psychonomic Monographs,* 1968, 2 (10, Whole No. 26).

15. Goodnow, The Nature of Intelligent Behavior, p. 172.

16. Ibid.

17. Ibid., p. 176.

18. Ibid.

19. Brown, A. L., and French, L. A. The Zone of Potential Development: Implications for Intelligence Testing in the Year 2000. In Sternberg, R. J. and Detterman, D. K. (eds.), *Human Intelligence,* Norwood: Ablex Publishing Corporation, 1979, p. 217-235.

20. Coles, G. S. The Learning-Disabilities Test Battery: Empirical and Social Issues, *Harvard Educational Review,* 1978, Vol. 48, No. 3, p. 313-340.

21. Goodnow, The Nature of Intelligent Behavior, p. 185.

22. Olson, D. R. The Languages of Instruction: The Literate Bias of Schooling. In Anderson, R. C., Spiro, R. J. and Montague, W. E. (eds.), *Schooling and the Acquisition of Knowledge.* New York: John Wiley and Sons, 1977, p. 65-89.

23. Ibid., p. 69.

24. Olson, D. R. From utterance to text: The bias of language in speech and writing. In Fisher, H. and Diez-Gurrero, R. (eds.), *Language and Logic in Personality and Society.* New York: Academic Press.

25. Olson, The Language of Instruction, p. 81-89.

26. Grover, S. C. Hypothesis formation as a facilitator of conceptual development. *Canadian Journal of Behavioral Science,* 1979, Vol. 11, No. 1, p. 53-63.

27. Olson, D. R. *Cognitive Development: The Child's Acquisition of Diagonality.* New York: Academic Press, 1970.

28. Ryan, W. *Blaming the Victim.* New York: Random House, 1971.

29. Feuerstein, R., Rand, Y., Hoffman, M., Hoffman, M., and Miller, R. Cognitive modifiability in retarded adolescents: Effects of instrumental enrichment. *American Journal of Mental Deficiency,* 1979, Vol. 83, No. 6, p. 539-550.

30. Jensen, A. R. How much can we boost I.Q. and scholastic achievement? *Harvard Educational Review,* 1969, 39, p. 1-123.

31. Jensen, A. R. Hierarchical Theories of Mental Ability. In Dockrell, W. B. (ed.), *On Intelligence,* London: Methuen, 1970.

CHAPTER SIX

INTELLECTUAL CAPACITY: STRUCTURAL LIMITATION OF THE BRAIN OR DYNAMIC PROCESS?

The evidence presented in this chapter is intended to support the contention that: "There is no real I.Q. inherent in the person, but only a variety of functions which may be measured in different ways . . . and yield various I.Q.'s" that are susceptible to varying degrees of modification (1, p. 146). Rejected is then the proposition that inherent in the individual is something roughly equivalent to general intelligence determined in large part by neural efficiency.

The notion that intellectual capacity correlates with some *structural* limitations in cognitive function which are genetically determined and unmodifiable will also be shown to be erroneous. The present author argues instead for a conception of intelligence as a *dynamic process.*

A view of intelligence as process would seem to be more in line with contemporary neuropsychological and cognitive findings. This research provides evidence for the possibility of partial or complete recovery of function in brain damaged individuals as the result of a variety of therapeutic environments as discussed in Chapter 2. As well, significant improvement in intellectual function has been demonstrated in retarded individuals whose cognitive strategies have been modified in relatively short periods, via experimental training techniques. Current psychometric measures of the intellect are not designed to assess or reflect such dynamic processes. Rather, these mental tests assess ability to produce a learned product (2), and provide little, if any, information as to process or changes in process. Such tests, furthermore, are not designed to assess ability to go beyond what is known already but rather tend to measure skills in exact reproduction of assimilated information.

Current psychometric measures purporting to assess the intellect are based on a view of intelligence as primarily cognitive in nature. The tests then fail to incorporate motivational and affective dimensions (3). The individual is viewed as an emotionless storehouse of information whose intelligence is manifested via the rapidity and degree of accuracy with which outputs can be produced. It is assumed that "The subject knows nothing of the (examiner's) intent and has no goals of his or her own to pursue. (However) in the real world, intelligence is as much problem finding as problem solving" (4, p. 196).

Examined in this chapter are aspects of a body of research on the training of the mentally retarded and mentally deficient. Some authors distinguish between these two categories, the latter category being more clearly associated with organic damage than the former (5) Much of the progress in modifying cognitive function in these individuals has resulted from a reconceptualization of intelligence as process rather than static entity. Concomitant with this new view has been a shift in emphasis from training simply for the acquisition of new information and skills to attempts also at modifying the thinking process itself. There has been then a growing recognition of the fact that intelligence is revealed "not by a commitment to fixed ideas, stereotyped procedure or immutable concepts, but by the manner in which, and the occasions on which changes in these ideas, procedures and concepts" are effected (6). The so-called intellectually subnormal have been found to be amenable to training aimed at modifying problem-solving approaches and definitions of problems. Before turning to an examination of such training studies, certain basic features of information-processing in the mentally retarded are presented in the next section.

Cognitive Process in the Mentally Retarded

Jensen, as was mentioned in the introduction, rejects a view of intelligence as involving learned strategies, for the latter he takes to be the "effect" of the former. Extent of transfer and rapidity with which new strategies are learned, he suggests, are dependent upon the immutable "g factor." He further contends that individual differences in mental test performance result from differences in the brain and not simply from how the brain is used. What these differences in the brain might be is never clearly outlined except for some vague indirect allusions to possibly greater complexity in neural networks among higher test scorers.

The evidence to be presented here suggests that whatever differences may exist in the brain of the mentally retarded individual, these are not sufficient to explain the differences in test performance. Rather, differences appear to be critically dependent upon experiential factors. The findings suggest that the basic structure of the processing system in the mentally retarded individual is, in many respects, essentially similar to that of the non-retarded (7). The potential for adequate intellectual function in various areas then appears to be present if proper training is provided.

Several studies reveal that short-term sensory storage processes are quite similar in both the retarded and nonretarded (8). For instance, rate of information loss from the sensory store has been found to be the same for both groups (9). When familiarity of stimuli is controlled,

73

similar rates of transfer of information from the sensory store to long-term memory have been demonstrated for both retarded and non-retarded groups (10,11).

Stanovich comments that "Though it would seem that most of the seminal studies of information processing in nonretarded adults have employed alphanumeric stimuli, one would not want to attribute a specific processing deficit to the retarded on the basis of studies using such stimuli" (12, p. 40). Unfortunately, processing deficits have been so attributed to the retarded without controlling for differential familiarity with the stimuli. For instance, studies which control for stimulus familiarity do not report the usual slower memory scanning rates for retarded subjects (13). Other evidence suggests that memory scanning (comparing a probe item to items in memory to determine membership in an arbitrarily defined positive set) is qualitatively similar in both groups. Both retarded and nonretarded individuals appear to employ a serial exhaustive memory scan.

Where differences do exist they appear due to a "lag in development of certain central processes, rather than a structural defect in . . . processing systems" (14, p. 55). Hence, while retarded persons may demonstrate slower same-different classification responses as well as slower responses to low probability stimuli, they often perform as do equal mental age nonretarded groups, providing evidence for developmental lag as a causal factor underlying inefficient processing (15).

It would seem that the concept of general intelligence is a mystical outdated one which was used to account for individual differences in functioning in various tasks before underlying processes could be adequately empirically investigated. The concept would seem to add

little to our understanding and has been, it is suggested, a major block to studies dealing with cognitive modifiability. Examined next are studies dealing with remediation of so-called intellectual deficiency.

Modifying the Intellect

Feuerstein distinguishes between distal and proximal etiology in retarded intellectual performance (16), a distinction which provides a useful framework for the discussion which follows. Distal determinants include, for example, genetic factors, organic pathology, socio-economic disadvantages. These factors are held to "neither directly nor inevitably result in retardation" (17, p. 540). However, such factors often lead to the triggering of proximal factors — that is, factors resulting in lack of mediated learning experiences. For instance, the genetically disordered Down's syndrome child may not receive adequate stimulation or structuring of stimulation from parent and/or teacher due to lack of information as to what is required to mitigate the child's learning difficulties. It would appear that mediated learning experiences are especially critical for the retarded, for these individuals appear often not to initiate learning strategies spontaneously and hence require training to do so. Further, the absence of appropriate strategies appears to underly much of their learning difficulty.

Studies seem to suggest that when a task does not involve active strategies, normal-retardate differences do not emerge nor do age-related trends in normals (18). Passivity in response to problem solving tasks appears to be not so much related to low intelligence, contrary to Jensen's contention, but rather to developmental immaturity. Hence, failure to spontaneously employ strategic cognitive behaviors in memory tasks, for instance, is not peculiar to the retarded but is also a common feature of the nonretarded young child's performance. In a study by Appel *et al* (19), for example, with normal preschool, first and fifth graders, only the older children employed active memory strategies such as rehearsal in a picture recall task. Younger children simply continued to passively look at the pictures even when instructions specified that they attempt to memorize them. With increasing age, however, the normal child appears to acquire active processing strategies and the retardate-normal differential on memory tasks requiring strategy use becomes more marked (20).

Retarded children have been found to demonstrate a deficiency in spontaneous strategy use in a wide range of tasks requiring a variety of strategies. Deficiencies in rehearsal, organizational strategies, associative clustering, and mnemonic elaboration have been demonstrated. Studies dealing with each are reviewed by Brown (21). The success of training the retarded in each of these areas suggests that failure to employ an appropriate strategy is open to remediation and does not reflect an immutable structural limitation.

Brown (22) reviews evidence suggesting that training the retarded to use rehearsal strategies results in patterns of performance similar to that of uninstructed equal-CA comparative groups. Of special interest is the finding that nonretarded individuals prevented from rehearsing show patterns similar to the untrained retarded subject (23). Variations in number of items which can be rehearsed as the result of training appear to be dependent upon the task and method of training as well as a host of additional factors.

It has been demonstrated that retardates do make use of organizational cues. Recall is enhanced, for example, if items are presented

76

clustered into conceptual categories or if presented unclustered but recall is requested by category (24). Brown suggests in view of this literature that, "It is the failure to spontaneously employ organizational strategies, rather than inability to use them, that is the main problem" (25, p. 380).

With respect to elaboration, retardates have also been shown to suffer from a "production deficiency" rather than a structural limitation preventing the use of mediators (26). For example, Milgram (27) trained retarded children to generate their own mediators using a fading technique, after first supplying mediators. The children were required to learn three paired-associate lists of nine picture pairs. List 3 was learned without supplied mediators and only the instruction to remember the earlier strategy. The mediation group learned faster overall than a group of controls. However, unlike controls, this mediation group showed no faster learning on later lists than earlier ones suggesting that these subjects had successfully generated useful mediators for the later list. Performance on List 3 was equal for retarded and nonretarded subjects in the mediation group. Hence, retarded individuals appear to be able to use elaboration strategies when trained to do so and go on to generate their own mediators as the result of such training.

Training for Transfer

Jensen argues that extent of transfer is a manifestation of the g factor and indicates that modification in intellectual function is limited by the same. While it is the case that transfer effects in many early training studies with the retarded were rather limited when gross changes in stimulus materials were made, this may have been due to the fact that metacognitive competencies were not also trained. For example, the subject is not trained to monitor his own use of a particular strategy. The subject may fail to persist in the use of a trained strategy if at some level he does not understand its value. Such, in fact, appears to have been the case for nonretarded children in a study by Kennedy and Miller (28) in which it was found that feedback as to the value of rehearsal was necessary to assure persistent use of the strategy.

Evidence from a study by Kendall *et al*, with retarded children suggests that metacognitive skills are an important determinant of extent of transfer. These researchers found that metamemory scores were significantly correlated with strategy use on maintenance and generalization tests leading them to suggest that "certain forms of metamemorial knowledge are not only predictors of, but also pre-requisites for, strategy generalization" (29, p. 269). As researchers begin to attempt to train metacognitive skills in the retarded and other learning impaired groups generalization effects should be greatly en-hanced.

Brown states that few, if any, studies have addressed the question of whether comparable training with nonretarded equal-CA groups would result in a reduction in individual differences between the retarded and nonretarded populations. She suggests that therefore "it is impossible to draw firm conclusions about the possible role of structural features" (30, p.396). This author contends, however, that even if training did not substantially reduce differences between retarded and nonretarded equal-CA groups, such would not necessarily implicate structural features as causative. It must be remembered that the retarded individual is likely to have suffered restricted opportunities for stimulating learning opportunities. Such individuals are often even quite unfamiliar with a range of social situations which the rest of us take for granted. It would then not be surprising, given the retarded individual's impoverished repertoire of skills and information, and possible motivational deficits, to find that less comprehensive training was not completely effective in eliminating deficiencies.

The retarded have had less practice than the intellectually normal in behaving intelligently for until recently they have not been provided the learning situations which would permit the same. Training studies have, however, demonstrated that it is possible to bring retarded individuals much closer than previously thought feasible to levels of performance in memory tasks, for example, which would be considered indicative of acceptable competencies in nonretarded equal-CA groups (e.g., 31). These findings then suggest that structural deficiency explanations are not always appropriate or necessary to account for retardate-normal performance differentials. Intellectual capacity is then better conceptualized as a dynamic process rather than synonymous with structural limitations in cognitive processes which are unmodifiable and biologically based.

REFERENCES

1. Cobb, H. V. *The Forecast of Fulfillment.* New York: Teachers' College Press, 1972.

2. Estes, W. K. Learning theory and intelligence. *American Psychologist,* October, 1973, p. 740-749.

3. Wechsler, D. Intelligence defined and undefined. *American Psychologist,* February, 1975, p. 135-139.

4. Snow, R. E. Intelligence for the Year 2001. *Intelligence,* 1980, 4, p.

185-199.

5. Thompson, R. T. Jr. and O'Quinn, A. N. *Developmental Disabilities.* New York: Oxford University Press, 1979.

6. Toulmin, S. *Human Understanding. Vol. 1: The Collective Use and Evolution of Concepts.* Princeton: Princeton University Press, 1972.

7. Stanovich, K. E. Information Processing in Mentally Retarded Individuals. In Ellis, N. R. (ed.), *International Review of Research in Mental Retardation:* Volume 9. New York: Academic Press, 1978.

8. Ibid.

9. Pennington, F. M. and Luszaz, M. A. Some functional properties of iconic storage in retarded and nonretarded subjects. *Memory and Cognition,* 1975, 3, p. 295-301.

10. Ryan, M. and Jones, B. Stimulus persistence in retarded and nonretarded children: A signal detection analyses. *American Journal of Mental Deficiency,* 1975, 80, p. 298-305.

11. Spitz, H. H. and Webreck, C. A. Effects of age and mental retardation on temporal integration of visual stimuli. *Perceptual and Motor Skills,* 1971, 33, p. 3-10.

12. Stanovich, Information Processing, p. 40.

13. Ibid., p. 46.

14. Ibid., p. 55.

15. Ibid.

16. Feuerstein, R., Rand, Y., Hoffman, M., Hoffman, M. and Miller, M. Cognitive modifiability in retarded adolescents: Effects of instrumental enrichment. *American Journal of Mental Deficiency,* 1979, 83, (6), p. 539-550.

17. Ibid., p. 540.

18. Brown, A. L. The Role of Strategic Behavior in Retardate Memory. In Ellis, N. R. (ed.), *International Review of Research in Mental Retardation,* Volume 7. New York: Academic Press, 1974.

19. Appel, L. F., Cooper, R. G., McCorrell, N., Sims-Knight, J., Yussen, S. R., and Flavell, J. H. The development of the distinction between perceiving and memorizing. *Child Development,* 1972, 43, p. 1365-1381.

20. Shif, Z. I. Development of Children in Schools for the Mentally Retarded. In Cole, M. and Maltzman (eds.), *A Handbook of Contemporary Soviet Psychology.* New York: Basic Books, 1969, p. 326-353.

21. Brown, Strategic Behavior in Retardate Memory, p. 55-111.

22. Ibid.

23. Brown, A. L., Campione, J. C., Bray, N. W. and Wilcox, B. L. Keeping track of changing variables: Effects of rehearsal training and rehearsal prevention in normal and retarded adolescents. *Journal of Experimental Psychology,* 1973, 101, p.123-131.

24. Gerjoy, I. R. and Spitz, H. Associative clustering in free recall: Intellectual and developmental variables. *American Journal of Mental Deficiency,* 1966, 70, p. 918-927.

25. Brown, Strategic Behavior in Retardate Memory, p. 380.

26. Borkowski, J. G. and Wanschura, P. B. Mediational Processes in the Retarded. In Ellis, N. R. (ed.), *International Review of Research in Mental Retardation,* Vol. 7. New York: Academic Press, 1974.

27. Milgram. N. A. Retention of mediation set in paired-associate learning of normal children and retardates. *Journal of Experimental Child Psychology,* 1967, 5, p. 341-349.

28. Kennedy, B. A. and Miller, D. J. Persistent use of verbal rehearsal as a function of information about its value. *Child Development,* 1976, 47, p. 566-569.

29. Kendall, C. R., Borkowski, J. G. and Cavanaugh, J. C. Metamemory and the transfer of an interrogative strategy by EMR children. *Intelligence,* 1980, 4, p. 255-270.

30. Campione, J. C. and Brown, A. L. Memory and Metamemory Development in Educable Retarded Children. In Kail, R. V. Jr. and Hagen, J. W. (eds.), *Perspectives on the Development of Memory and Cognition.* New York: John Wiley and Sons, 1977.

31. Belmont, J. M. and Butterfield, E. C. Learning strategies as determinants of memory deficiencies. *Cognitive Psychology,* 1971, 2, p. 411-420.

CHAPTER SEVEN

PROBLEMS IN THE ASSESSMENT OF THE COGNITIVE BASIS OF LEARNING DIFFICULTIES

Assessing Individual Differences

> If there were no biological diversity we would not need legal civil liberties, because it is easy to afford rights to those who are most like us . . . (there are those) whose fears for such rights tempt them to suppress the truth about human differences (1, p. 341).

This temptation, it is hoped, has been avoided by this author. The attempt has been not to deny individual differences in learning, but to examine possible underlying mechanisms thereof, appropriate assessment strategies, and the question of cognitive modifiability.

It is odd that proponents of I.Q. testing (for selection purposes and so on) should present themselves as realists: purveyors of the well kept secret that individual differences exist. In fact, the psychometric movement has done little to further understanding of the mechanisms underlying such differences: "little progress has been made thus far in understanding mental abilities in terms of processes" (2, p. 88).

Process-oriented studies of cognitive psychologists appear to hold some promise in this regard and are discussed in some detail in Chapter 11. Information-processing approaches are not, however, without their own complex conceptual and methodological difficulties. For instance:

> There has been some success in identifying psychological processes, but the interpretation of these processes often stands or falls

depending upon whether one can accept the information-processing models on which the identification of a particular process is based (3, p. 88).

Often individual differences isolated in such studies are task-specific rather than general (4, p. 88). This poses a problem for theorists who, unlike this author, hold to notions of general intelligence. Further, as Carroll points out, there is a danger of "circularity in associating 'traits' (or 'abilities') *inferred* from psychometric tests with processes 'defined largely on the basis of those traits' " (5, p. 88). It should also be noted that finding individual differences in process variables, such as efficiency in encoding stimuli, between persons with different scores on aptitude tests does not ipso facto provide evidence for the role of intelligence in this individual variation. Maturational, cultural, instructional variables; as well as others, may also be implicated to a greater or lesser degree (6, p. 298).

Carroll provides an extensive review of statistical methodological problems which have plagued studies aimed at relating psychometrically-defined individual traits and abilities with process variables identified via experimental cognitive tasks (7). These difficulties include, for example, the use of simple correlational techniques which may mask additional sources of variance. Controversy also surrounds the uses and interpretations given factor analytic data in such work. One important study by Hunt *et. al.,* for instance, which purported to demonstrate some of the processes underlying high verbal intelligence has been challenged on the grounds that: "the purely 'verbal' tests had no significant loadings on the factors that were chiefly associated with the information-processing tasks" (8, p. 101). Others have defended vigorously the validity of these statistical techniques and the data interpretations arising from them (9).

The encouraging aspect of these general research trends is the shifting of focus from an exclusive preoccupation with psychometric traits and abilities, to a consideration of process variables and their implications for notions of individual difference in intelligence.

Some Negative Consequences Arising from the Psychometric Approach to the Question of Individual Difference

I.Q. Testing and the Mentally Retarded

The psychometric approach to individual differences in learning and performance has tended to mask the enormous variability that exists at every I.Q. level (10). This is particularly unfortunate in that those persons who tend to be more variable, such as the retarded, are precisely those who also tend to be most frequently labelled and rigidly categorized according to I.Q. level. Such classification procedures often seem to generate fairly uniform expectations among many of those who train and care for the retarded. This is to be expected given the rather crude classification system that I.Q. tests entail. Individualized program strategies are likely to be rather predictably poor as a result, if they exist at all.

Treating the mentally handicapped as a homogeneous group is a frequent consequence of the use of I.Q. tests despite the fact that: "I.Q. tests do not provide information as to whether processes underlying performance deficits on particular tests are the same in this heterogeneous group or whether they differ" (11, p. 42). Indeed, labels referring to retardation appear to be "meaningless for the purposes of behavioral analysis" (12, p. 41). It would seem then that I.Q. testing has little implication in terms of providing adequate predictions of some specificity regarding performance on particular tasks for this group. Hence, the use of such tests cannot be easily justified on the basis of diagnostic value or use in planning remedial programs in this instance.

I.Q. Testing and the "Learning Disabled"

The so-called "learning disabled" individual who experiences significant learning problems in one or more areas, despite an average or above average I.Q. score, presents a number of conceptual challenges to those who support models of general intelligence. This because a concept of average general intelligence implies adequate learning skills on a range of tasks; barring confounding factors such as cultural deprivation. The phenomenon of learning disability as currently defined is difficult to accommodate via models of general intelligence which tend to ignore such individual differences in learning skills.

A learning disability is most often defined as "a disorder manifested by a difficulty in learning . . . despite conventional instruction, adequate intelligence and sociocultural opportunity" (13, p. 12). Most often the definition also excludes persons suffering from sensory deficit, emotional handicap, or clearly identifiable neurologic disorder. The term is fraught with conceptual inconsistencies for it is unclear, for instance, what defines adequate intelligence, conventional or appropriate instruction and sufficient sociocultural opportunity (14). The concept of learning disability furthermore tends to focus attention almost entirely upon the individual rather than upon student-teacher interaction patterns. Judgments regarding student learning potential and problems thus tend to be made out of context (15).

At present, I.Q. testing is an essential aspect of the diagnosis of learning disability in that a specified deviance between actual achievement levels (e.g., in school) versus those levels predicted on the basis of the I.Q. score serves as the major diagnostic criterion. Errors of misclassification are inevitable using such an unsophisticated methodology. The weaknesses of such a discrepancy definition of learning disability have been critically analyzed by Shepard (16).

It appears then that the I.Q. test has played a central role in the invention of this new "syndrome." A child with normal intelligence who does not profit adequately from conventional, instructional techniques aimed at the mass of students runs the high risk of being regarded as learning disabled. One of the assumptions underlying the I.Q. test is that everyone ought to be able to learn the same things in the same way. Once again the I.Q. test, linked with a network of assumptions, has served to negate and hinder understanding of individual variation, for instance, in student instructional needs and modes of learning. This because the test assists in labelling as disabled those who learn by alternative modes. This is not to deny that there exist inefficient learners. Rather, it is here suggested that many students are being mislabeled as learning disabled simply because an educational system, which adopts the assumptions underlying I.Q. tests, tends to also hold that all students must learn by standard means. Tolerable ranges in individual differences in this regard are severely constrained.

It is important to note that while I.Q. tests are used to "screen out" the learning disabled and distinguish them from other diagnostic groups, the distinctions would appear to have little independent empirical support. For instance, there has been much controversy about whether the learning disabled individual is distinguishable from the retarded individual with such learning problems (17, p. 15). Often the retarded individual has severe learning problems not predictable on the basis of his MA (18), yet such an individual is excluded from the category of the learning disabled by definition. Whether the learning problems are qualitatively different for these various groups is also not clear. There is some suggestive evidence that learning disabled children are deficient in cognitive strategies just as are the retarded (19, p. 455).

A definition of learning disability in terms of deviance from predicted potential achievement levels estimated on the basis of I.Q. scores has led to a tendency to regard the learning disabled as a homogeneous group. One "important reason for dissatisfaction with the 'classic' definitions (of learning disability) is that they assume . . . a single syndrome" (20, p. 455). Yet, for individuals with severe reading problems, for instance, "there is little evidence for homogeneity . . . with respect to the qualitative aspects of . . . performance, the status of other cognitive functions, their history, or their neurological condition" (21, p. 456).

In sum, it would appear that, rather than foster a greater appreciation and understanding of individual difference variables, as Jensen claims, the psychometric approach has often led to a neglect of such factors. General I.Q. measures often are used to categorize persons into artificially defined groups, presumed homogeneous in terms of intellectual level, but in fact consisting of enormous variation between individuals within the group. Such measures also provide little or no insight into process variables underlying such individual differences.

Psychometric Measures Versus "Training-Tests"

What is suggested here is that adequate assessment of specific intellectual skills may necessitate the use of "training-tests" rather than psychometric measures which assess acquired skills and ability to produce what is already known and not the learning process itself. The training-test in contrast assesses, for example, changes in rate of learning, mode of optimal learning and so on. Such measures may also permit assessment of the individual's ability to profit from instruction as a function of his skill in monitoring his own learning process. As discussed previously in Chapter 6, research with the retarded has suggested that deficiencies in strategic behaviors are an essential causative factor in the performance deficiencies of the retarded. It appears that the retarded performer may often have the components of a strategy available, but does not combine these appropriately nor perceive the need for the application of such strategies (22, p. 288). In the view of Campione and Brown "Intelligence differences are attributable to variations in the efficiency of the executive, or in the quality of control that executive exerts" (23, p. 293). In other words, the intelligent individual, according to this view, is one who understands his own cognitive limitations on particular tasks and can make use of what is known and of strategic skills to compensate for these deficiencies, to a degree, so as to improve his learning.

The work of Feuerstein (24) is a step in the direction of "training-tests," but there is little comparable work carried out in North America. Such an approach would not allow for holding the individual completely accountable for his test performance as is now (unfairly) the case with I.Q. tests. It would become evident, it is here claimed, with training tests that test performance (as with *any* test) is not simply a function of "god-given" strengths and limitations in ability, but also of the effectiveness of the training afforded the individual. Such training tests should also assist in eliminating some of the oversimplifications arising from the notions of "structure" and "process." It should become more evident through their use that such distinctions are most often impossible to make. Predictions based upon assumptions regarding the structural limitations of an individual's information processing skills must therefore be considered as tenuous at best.

It should be noted that structural differences with regard to information-processing between individuals of different I.Q. levels (as assessed by a general I.Q. test) have not been adequately established (25). Rather, at present, the evidence could more easily be interpreted in terms of differences in modifiable process variables such as strategies for allocation of attention (26). It would seem that psychometric I.Q. tests have, to a certain extent, been "falsely advertised" as assessing performance differentials that reflect stable, structural differences between individuals. Attempts to link process variables to psychometric I.Q. test factors, it is here claimed, are based on the fallacious assumption that any such correlations would reveal the stable, structural basis of the process differences. However, such correlations would add little, if anything, to our understanding of the mechanisms underlying individual differences in information processing. They would, of course, appear (falsely) to reify hypothetical psychometric factors derived via controversial statistical techniques.

Summary

It has here been argued that psychometric testing approaches have done much to mask significant individual variations while providing little, if any, information as to their underlying mechanisms. Yet the use of such tests for selection purposes is often staunchly defended (27) on the erroneous grounds that it is by means of such tests that individual differences can be meaningfully assessed. Scarr suggests further that "their abolishment will not revolutionize anyone's life chances" (28, p. 327). This author suggests that while eliminating their use for selection purposes may not revolutionize anyone's life chances (as social inequity has many causes), this would certainly be a step in the direction of greater social justice. It is inordinately naive, it is here argued, that Scarr should hold that "the use of I.Q. tests for selection of educational and occupational elites need not lead inexorably to social and economic elites" (29, p. 341). I.Q. tests have served to legitimize the current distribution of wealth (30). A socially equitable distribution of wealth is not likely as long as psychometric tests are used to support the empirically indefensible meritocratic principle that social class differences reflect, for the most part, inherent differences in cognitive capacities as assessed by the I.Q. test.

To reject the value of I.Q. tests for selection purposes on conceptual, moral and empirical grounds is not at all to deny biological diversity as Scarr suggests it is. Rather, it is to recognize that psychometric I.Q. tests are not an adequate means for assessing that biological diversity. Such tests do not significantly further understanding of the process variables underlying individual variations among persons at the same I.Q. level. The classification which results in fact often serves to mask such variations. In addition, individual profiles on many of the mental measures (e.g. WISC) are notoriously unreliable in any case (31). Variations within individuals across a variety of tasks are clarified little via the use of psychometric tests. Further, the possible alternative strategies and cognitive processes used by different persons to produce the same performance outcome or by the same person at different developmental periods are not clarified by such assessment procedures. In general, psychometric measures of general intelligence do much to cloud the whole issue of individual difference and add little to its elucidation.

A reemphasis upon process variables underlying individual differences in test performance is needed. Training tests may serve to provide such a focus and can be used, as Estes recommended intelligence tests be employed, to indicate the steps that ought to be taken to improve intellectual performance, rather than being used to predict "intellectual performance" (32).

REFERENCES

1. Scarr, S. From evaluation to Larry P., or what shall we do about I.Q. tests? *Intelligence,* 1978, 2, p. 325-342.
2. Carroll, J. B. How shall we study individual differences in cognitive abilities? Methodological and theoretical perspectives. *Intelligence,* 1978, 2, p. 87-115.
3. Ibid., p. 88.
4. Ibid.
5. Ibid.

6. Campione, J. C. and Brown, A. L. Toward a theory of intelligence: contributions from research with retarded children. *Intelligence,* 1978, 2, p. 279-304.

7. Carroll, Individual differences in cognitive abilities, p. 87-115.

8. Ibid., p. 101.

9. Jarman, R. F. Comments on John B. Carrol's "How shall we study individual differences in cognitive abilities? Methodological and theoretical perspectives." *Intelligence,* 1980, 4, p. 73-82.

10. Ryan, J. Scientific research and individual variation. In Clarke, A. D. B. and Clarke, A. M. (eds.) *Mental Retardation and Behavioral Research.* Study Group No. 4. London: Churchill Livingston, 1973, p. 23-30.

11. Ellis, N. R. Do the mentally retarded have poor memory? *Intelligence,* 1978, 2, p. 41-54.

12. Ibid., p. 41.

13. Rutter, M. Prevalence and Types of Dyslexia. In Benton, A. L. and Pearl, D. (eds.), *Dyslexia: An Appraisal of Current Knowledge.* New York: Oxford University Press, 1978, p. 5-28.

14. Ibid.

15. Grover, S. C. Learning disabilities: cause for concern. *Canada's Mental Health* (in press).

16. Shepard, L. An evaluation of the regression discrepancy method for identifying children with learning disabilities. *The Journal of Special Education,* 1980, 14(1), p. 79-91.

17. Rutter, Prevalence and types of dyslexia, p. 5-28.

18. Benton, A. Some Conclusions about Dyslexia. In Benton and Pearl (eds.) *Dyslexia,* p. 453-476.

19. Loper, A. R. Metacognitive development: implications for cognitive training. *Exceptional Education Quarterly,* 1980, p. 1-8.

20. Benton, Some Conclusions about Dyslexia. In Benton and Pearl (eds.) *Dyslexia,* p. 455.

21. Ibid., p. 456.

22. Campione and Brown, Toward a theory of intelligence, p. 279-304.

23. Ibid., p. 293.

24. Feuerstein, R. In collaboration with Rand, Y. and Hoffman, M. B. *The Dynamic Assessment of Retarded Performers.* Baltimore: University Press, 1979.

25. Ellis, Do the mentally retarded have poor memory? p. 4-54.

26. Yeaman, D. Some relations of general intelligence and selective attention. *Intelligence,* 1978, 2, p. 55-73.

27. Scarr, What shall we do about I.Q. tests? p. 325-342.

28. Ibid., p. 327.

29. Ibid., p. 341.

30. Bowles, S. and Gintis, H. I.Q. in the U.S. class structure. *Social Policy,* 1973, 3, p. 65-96.

31. Ross, A. *Psychological Aspects of Learning Disabilities and Reading Disorders.* New York: McGraw-Hill, 1976.

32. Estes, W. K. Learning theory and intelligence. *American Psychologists,* October 1974, p. 740-749.

CHAPTER EIGHT

BIAS IN MENTAL TESTING — MYTH OR REALITY?

External Validity

Jensen claims that current mental tests are unbiased measures both for minority group members and members of the Anglo majority. He bases this claim on the finding of equivalent validity coefficients across "racial" groups. He further points to the results of regression studies which suggest current mental measures generally overpredict criterion performance for blacks when a common regression line is used for scores combined from both groups (1, p. 515). The single regression line based on combined scores generally falls above that of the line for the black group alone, the latter having a lower intercept than the regression line for whites alone. The argument Jensen is putting forth, in sum, is that the tests are fair because they predict equally well for both groups and, if anything, overestimate criterion performance for blacks. The issue of why mean scores for blacks are lower than those for whites is regarded by Jensen as irrelevant with regard to the issue of test bias. He states, " . . . the presence of population differences in the distribution of test scores is not by itself a proper criterion for judging test bias . . . " (2, p. 11).

The case Jensen is making is in its logical form akin to affirming the consequent — assuming that accurate conclusions (predictions) somehow validate the premises from which those (predictions) were derived. However, it seems to be the case instead that scores derived from *faulty* measures of the intellect are being used to predict criterion performance. That certain positive correlations between such measures and criterion performance do exist does not bear on the issue of whether current mental tests accurately assess the intellect. Predictive validity provides no ipso facto evidence for construct validity. To illustrate the point, imagine predicting school performance and other socially relevant variables on the basis of color or ethnic origin alone. No doubt the predictions would be relatively accurate. It can be stated that intelligence tests operate in precisely this fashion. Mercer (3), for example, found that the more an individual's life style conformed to that of the Anglo majority, the higher his I.Q. score. Hence, measures of the intellect appear to predict criterion performance by screening for cultural differences, not intelligence.   Predictive power is taken by proponents of current mental measures to be an indicator that the tests assess skills of some relevance and equivalence of validity coefficients is held to suggest that the measure is unbiased. Statistically the argument is flawless, but conceptually It Is meaningless for current mental tests have little or no construct validity. Tests are biased in a non-statistical sense to the degree that they place certain individuals or groups at an unfair systematic disadvantage. The fact is that more minority group members do poorly on current "mental" tests of dubious construct validity and as a result are denied various academic, and occupational opportunities. The deficiency, test authors and users claim, is in the individual not in the test or the society at large. Yet this claim has not been put to empirical test. What is suggested here is that current mental tests measure the results of social injustice (e.g., poor academic instruction) and predict to a degree the long term effects of that injustice.

It ought to be mentioned that the predictive validity of current mental measures, unconfounded by other variables, is often exaggerated. With social class controlled, for instance, I.Q. test performance is a poor predictor of occupational success (4). Achievement tests are much better predictors of school performance than are general I.Q. tests (5).

Jensen has, it would seem, defined away the issue of test bias by viewing it "as a technical matter concerned with correlation coefficients, regression lines, and intercepts, (having) dismissed questions about . . . assumptions as 'irrelevant nonscientific debate' " (6, p. 15). Why mean test scores for white versus black groups differ is held to be irrelevant to the question of test bias, Jensen holds. That I.Q. tests measure "pure" intellect accurately is taken primarily on faith. Given all of those assumptions, it is quite unclear what equivalence of validity coefficients across groups signifies. While such equivalence may rule out test bias in a statistical sense, it does not rule out the possibility that the tests are *unfair*; that is, that they result in unjust discrimination based upon *inferred* deficiencies in intellectual competence and the faulty assumption that minority group members have been afforded equal opportunity and been found wanting. So it is that the issue of the external validity of mental measures remains unresolved despite Jensen's definitive statements to the contrary.

Internal Validity

The issue of what it is mental tests purportedly measure was discussed in Chapter 4. It was concluded, on the basis of a review of cognitive and neuropsychological research, that they do not measure significant cognitive process. In this respect, then, the tests lack internal validity. Jensen, however, makes an additional argument for internal validity of mental measures aside from his suggestion that correlations of I.Q., reaction time, and evoked potentials etcetera demonstrate that the tests assess biologically based intellectual skills. He argues that such tests are culture fair. Jensen contends that, for instance, rank order of item difficulties are dissimilar in two disparate groups on culturally biased tests but not on culture fair tests such as the WISC. (7). Mercer notes, however, that:

> No rationale is presented to support the postulate. No data are presented which demonstrate even a single case in which measures of internal validity, such as the rank order of item difficulty or the types of errors made in answering questions, are correlated with the sociocultural characteristics of persons taking the tests . . . (8, p. 13).

It appears that Jensen often puts forth nonempirically based assumptions in the debate concerning the validity of psychometric measures which are to be taken on faith in his view. Jensen has thus formulated a set of criteria which are to be used in determining the validity of mental measures. Many of these criteria have no empirical foundation, as with the notion that internally valid tests result in similar ordering of item difficulties for culturally disparate groups. Other criteria have no adequate theoretical basis other than the fact that they serve well certain political ideologies as, for example, the notion that correlations of test scores with school achievement and occupational success attest to the external validity of the measures. Nowhere is it explained "*who decides* which performances are significant, relevant and important (in determining external validity of tests). Such decisions are political not scientific" (9, p. 9). One is led to conclude that bias in mental testing is less of a myth and more of a reality than Jensen would suggest.

REFERENCES

1. Jensen, A.R. *Bias in Mental Testing.* New York: The Free Press, 1980, p. 515.

2. Ibid., p. 11.

3. Mercer, J. A policy statement on assessment procedures and the rights of children. *Harvard Educational Review,* 1974, 44(1), p. 125-141.

4. Bowles, S. and Gintis, H. I.Q. in the United States class structure. *Social Policy,* 3, Nos. 4 and 5, 1972/73.

5. Bloom, B. *Human Characteristics and School Learning.* New York: McGraw-Hill, 1976.

6. Mercer, J. Test validity, bias and fairness: An analysis from the perspective of the sociology of knowledge. *Interchange,* 1978-79, 9(1), p. 1-16.

7. Jensen, A.R. Test bias and construct validity. Invited address presented at the 83rd Annual Convention of the American Psychological Association, Chicago, September, 1975.

8. Mercer, Test validity, bias and fairness: An analysis from the perspective of the sociology of knowledge, p. 13.

9. Ibid., p. 9.

CHAPTER NINE

SCIENTISTS AND SOCIAL JUSTICE

Jensen's Claims

Jensen contends that the power of mental tests to discriminate, in a statistical sense, does not necessarily carry with it any particular social policy implications such as discriminatory practices as normally understood (1, p. 44). These policy consequences, he claims, will be solely dependent upon how it is decided to employ mental measures. He goes on to argue that tests can be used to promote social justice in a manner which is much more efficient than any strategy which could be devised that did not include what he views as the objective, empirical evidence regarding competencies provided by mental measures.

Jensen defends against the charge that mental tests, as currently designed and employed, serve well racist ideologies by asserting that "the well established finding of a wide range of individual differences in I.Q. and other abilities within all major racial populations and the great amount of overlap of their frequency distributions, absolutely contradicts the racist philosophy that persons of different races should be treated differently, one and all, only by reason of their racial origins" (2, p. 738). He claims then that mental measures shift the focus away from racial groups "as a criterion to selection on the basis of *individual* talents and abilities" (3, p. 740).

Jensen suggests further that since ours is a society of competition, there is a need for a rational approach to selection. "The only question then is *how* to discriminate" (4, p. 51). He agrees that mental measures

101

have done little to promote the social advancement of black Americans and quotes Jencks who stressed that a system which deemphasizes cognitive skills would be of greater advantage to blacks (5, p. 51).

Critique of Jensen's Position on Mental Measures as Promoters of the Social Good

Jensen in his text, "Bias in Mental Testing," skillfully argues in favor of the meritocratic philosophy. He claims that he need not and will not allude in his text to the causes of differences in scores between "racial" groups on various mental measures. However, to attribute these differences in test scores between "racial groups" to cognitive abilities as does Jensen *is* to make a causal analysis. Differences in performance ought not be automatically equated with differences in abilities, yet this is precisely the equivalence which Jensen presumes to be the case. No longer does Jensen speak forthrightly about the presumed genetically based mental inferiority of blacks as he did in earlier works (6), yet neither is there a retraction of his earlier views. He implies that the meritocratic philosophy emphasizes the development of *individual* talents and that mental tests operate so as to discover these independent of group membership. Jensen adroitly argues that "it has been practically axiomatic among people in the testing field that the fact of statistical differences between racial populations should not be permitted to influence the treatment accorded *individuals* of any race — in education, employment, legal justice and political and civil rights" (7, p. 737). One wonders how "axiomatic" it could have been, given that Jensen himself suggested that individuals who do poorly on I.Q. tests, as often do certain minority group individuals from lower socio-economic classes, cannot be expected to acquire certain higher level skills and that educational efforts not be concentrated in that direction.

For Jensen, "the only question is how to discriminate" in a competitive society. It is not at all clear, however, that this is *the* question to be asked. An equally legitimate question would seem to be "How to assure that every individual participates fully in a democratic society, economically and politically." That selection in the distribution of the good things of life should be of prime concern to Jensen is a reflection of his meritocratic ideology which is dedicated to assuring a stratified society based on criteria allegedly adequate to establish merit. Jensen betrays his basic orientation when he states that I.Q. testing is not critical for elementary school children as there is no selection problem at that stage given the existence of compulsory education for all (8, p. 716). What then of the use of tests for the development of individual talents which he claims is a priority of the meritocratic philosophy? Given all of the aforementioned, it seems misleading at best that Jensen should suggest that the widespread use of mental measures does not imply any concomitant specific approach to social policy matters.

Jensen charges that "sympathy for the less fortunate may prompt acceptance of criticisms of tests without evidence" (9, p. 23). Here he is arguing then that opponents of a selection process based on the results of mental tests are simply naive, soft-hearted liberals unable to face the stark reality that individual differences do exist. He has, however, missed the point that most of those "unfortunates" were socially created using an unsound methodology for selection.

Social Class and Opportunity in a Society
Enamoured with the I.Q.

According to Jensen, I.Q. neatly corresponds to the level of attainment which can be expected of an individual. He states:

> The importance of a given difference (in I.Q.) depends not only on its magnitude but on whether or not it crosses over any of the social, educational and occupational thresholds of I.Q. Such probabilistic thresholds are not established by arbitrary convention or definition but reflect the structure of the educational, and occupational systems of modern industrial society and their correlated demands on the kind of cognitive ability measured by I.Q. tests (10, p. 114).

This is a most extraordinary claim given that it is not at all clear what cognitive abilities the I.Q. test does or does not measure as has been discussed, nor whether whatever it measures is relevant to educational or occupational success, a topic to be considered next.

Bowles and Gintis (11) present evidence which suggests that in fact I.Q. has very little to do directly with occupational or educational success. These authors demonstrated that "for a given level of social background and schooling, differences in I.Q. add very little to the ability to predict eventual economic success" (12, p. 72). I.Q. appears to be related to economic success, Bowles and Gintis argue, via the effects of the correlated variables — years of schooling and social class background. But is this not simply because schools gradually select out individuals with higher I.Q.'s with the result that individuals with more years of schooling possess higher I.Q.'s and so also the requisite cognitive capacities for greater economic success? Bowles and Gintis counter this view with empirical evidence that individuals with similar adult I.Q.'s, but differing levels of schooling, have substantially different chances of economic success. From this data, the authors conclude "schooling affects chances of economic success predominately by the non-cognitive traits which it generates or on the basis of which it selects individuals for higher education" (13, p. 72). Traits such as compliance are essential in this process in the view of Bowles and Gintis.

Jensen, however, claims that those who succeed in our society are most often the brightest. He cites Cronbach's table purporting to show I.Q. levels most typical for individuals in various occupational and social class groups with steady increases for the upper classes and/or more educated groups (14, p. 113). In addition he claims, citing the work of Cox, that the majority of eminent men in history "would likely have been recognized as gifted in childhood if they had been given an I.Q. test" (15, p. 113). Jensen relies then upon basically methodologically unsound studies, studies involving retrospective analyses and upon faulty argument to make his claims relating to I.Q. and social class.

Blum offers an incisive critique of the "science" of historiometry that pertains to the Cox research which Jensen cites. Blum states: "The early proponents of I.Q. tests judiciously neglected to administer them to eminent artists and scientists who were living, instead they had themselves estimated the I.Q.'s of geniuses who were deceased . . . The raters all believed that I.Q. scores were a measure of capacity for intellectual accomplishment so they interpreted any significant achievement as *prima facie* evidence of a very high score" (16, p. 73). This surely is a good example of the circular argumentation which is fairly common among those who argue for the I.Q. test as an accurate measure of cognitive potential. Blum continues:

> Similar methods could be used with as much justification to demonstrate that mental capacity depends primarily on amount of alcohol consumed. The liquor industry could hire five of its spokesmen to estimate the drinking habits of 300 deceased geniuses . . . the spokesmen would comb through biographies and historical records for any evidence of alcohol consumption. Such evidence would then be exaggerated and interpreted as proof that the artists and scientists in question were habitual drunkards . . . since these estimates were based on lack of information, they could be safely revised upward, given the shared faith in the magical, stimulating properties of alcohol (17, p. 74).

Jensen, as an advocate of the meritocratic state, claims that mental measures can be reliably used for selection purposes such that society will gradually be stratified according to merit; with the elites being more cognitively capable than those at the lower echelons of the structure. As has been emphasized, the claims of the meritocratic philosopher are not founded upon empirical evidence, they can be safely added to the list of the metaphysical assumptions already discussed in Chapter 3. To make the point yet more forcefully, consider the case of the S.A.T. (Scholastic Aptitude Test) and its whole-hearted endorsement by Jensen (18, p. 726) and other meritocratic ideologists.

The S.A.T. is considered by its developers to be a measure of learning potential and not simply another achievement test. Supporters of the test argue it is a valid measure of basic aptitude and as such is unaffected by training designed to boost scores (19). Jensen seems to suggest that the S.A.T. is a psychometric marvel; permitting a matching between individual capabilities and particular college standards. The use of the S.A.T. has made it the case, according to Jensen, that "The saying that to find a college suitable for every level of ability is only a slight exaggeration" (20, p. 483).

Jensen notes that only 45 per cent of all high school seniors obtain S.A.T. verbal scores of 400 or more and only 20 per cent above 500; while the corresponding estimates for blacks are 15 per cent and 1 or 2 per cent, respectively (21, p. 483). He further states that what bias exists in S.A.T. scores works in favor of black students by overpredicting their probable first year college grades (22, p. 486). Jensen discounts completely the possibility of significant training effects on the S.A.T. (23, p. 592). The issue is a critical one in that an aptitude test ought not to be affected significantly by previous experience and/or training, lest it become but a measure of acquired skills. Slack and Porter (24) review empirical studies on the effects of coaching upon S.A.T. scores. Contrary to the claims of Jensen and the Educational Testing Service, these authors found that training with relevant material in the school setting often has significant effects upon S.A.T. performance. Gains reported by E.T.S. as the result of coaching are about equivalent to score differences between students accepted or rejected by their preferred college. Hence, it is quite clear that the differences produced by coaching are not only statistically significant, but also would be of great personal consequence to the students involved.

The S.A.T. is a relatively poor predictor of college grades, yet it is purported by Jensen and others to be an indispensable device for discriminating between those who are good versus poor academic risks for particular colleges. S.A.T. validities for recent years . . . average about .40 for S.A.T.-V, .35 for S.A.T.-M, with .50 for H.S.R. (high school record) and .58 for the combined predictors (25). Slack and Porter (26, p. 165) point out that these correlations represent but an increase of .08 in the predictive validity coefficient afforded by the high school record alone. Clearly, there are nonscientific reasons which account for the emphasis placed upon the S.A.T. by many American universities. The increase in predictive power using the S.A.T. simply does not provide any empirical justification for such a reliance upon S.A.T. scores as a criterion in college admission. The reduction in errors of prediction as the result of using the S.A.T. ranges from 2 per cent to 6 per cent, depending on the particular forecasting index used (27, p. 157). There is, in addition, considerable evidence that the correlation of achievement test scores with college grades are significantly greater than are correlations between college grades and S.A.T. scores (28).

There is, then, no convincing empirical evidence that the S.A.T. measures basic abilities or learning potential, nor that it predicts college grades adequately. The effects of training are substantial yet systematically downplayed by promoters of the test. The studies on training which have been conducted by promoters of the test have tended to be seriously flawed methodologically as for example, the study by Coffman and Parry (29) in which college students were tested on the S.A.T. before and after a speed reading course. It is, of course, quite questionable as to whether a speed reading course is relevant to the task demands of the S.A.T. (30).

It is noteworthy that in general promulgators of psychometric aptitude measures have not tended to investigate thoroughly the effects of training. To recognize the substantial effects of training on alleged measures of intellect or aptitude would be to render the test trivial. It should be mentioned that several authors have demonstrated substantial gains on other types of aptitude tests as well, including the Ravens, an allegedly culture-reduced test which should be quite resistant to training effects (31).

Given the weaknesses of the S.A.T., and the lack of empirical evidence in support of claims as to its predictive and construct validity, those who have promoted its use for selection purposes have served to perpetuate certain myths regarding the power of such tests. A similar process has functioned to assure the widespread use of the I.Q. tests in elementary school when, in fact, achievement tests are better predictors of future school performance than are general intellectual measures (32).

Jensen would have us make critical decisions about others' lives using so-called aptitude tests with dubious predictive validity and little, if any, face validity. Actual performance in the life situations most closely related to those in which performance is to be predicted are devalued. Substituted as a basis for prediction are artificial, contrived settings and tasks which, for a good proportion of minority group members, result in the denial of those opportunities that ought to be afforded them. Thus it happens, for example, that "the black law student who successfully completed all his own courses through . . . law school suddenly finds that he is unable to pass that one final examination that permits him to engage in his chosen profession" (33). This denial of opportunity is rationalized in terms of presumed cognitive deficiency in the candidate and the status quo wittingly or unwittingly is effectively maintained as a result. It is indeed tragic that those who do poorly on such mental tests need to be reminded that a low score is "unrelated to the quality of their minds" (34).

REFERENCES

1. Jensen, A. R. *Bias in Mental Testing*. New York: The Free Press, 1980, p. 44.
2. Ibid., p. 738.
3. Ibid., p. 740.
4. Ibid., p. 51.
5. Ibid., p. 51.
6. Jensen, A. R. How much can we boost I.Q. *Harvard Educational Review*, 1969, 39, p. 1-123.
7. Jensen, Bias in Mental Testing, p. 737.
8. Ibid., p. 716.
9. Ibid., p. 23.
10. Ibid., p. 114.
11. Bowles, S. and Gintis, H. I.Q. in the U.S. class structure. *Social Policy*, Nov.-Dec. 1972, p. 65-96.
12. Ibid., p. 72.
13. Ibid.
14. Jensen, *Bias in Mental Testing*, p. 113.
15. Ibid., p. 113.
16. Blum, M. *Pseudoscience and Mental Ability*. New York: Monthly Review Press, 1978, p. 73.
17. Ibid., p. 74.
18. Jensen, *Bias in Mental Testing*, p. 726.
19. Alderman, D. L. and Powers, D. E. The effect of special preparation on S.A.T. verbal scores (RDR 78-79, No. 4). Princeton: Educational Testing Service, 1979.
20. Jensen, *Bias in Mental Testing*, p. 483.

21. Ibid.

22. Ibid., p. 486.

23. Ibid., p. 592.

24. Slack, W. N. and Porter, D. The scholastic aptitude test: A critical appraisal. *Harvard Educational Review,* 1980, 50(2), p. 154-175.

25. Ford, S. F. and Campos, S. Summary of Validity Data from the Admissions Testing Program Validity Study Service, Princeton: College Entrance Examination Board, 1977.

26. Slack, and Porter, The scholastic aptitude test, p. 165.

27. Ibid., p. 157.

28. Coffman, W. E. The Achievement Tests. In W. H. Angoff (ed.), The College Board Admissions Testing Program. New York: College Entrance Examination Board, 1971.

29. Coffman, W. E. and Parry, M. E. Effects of an accelerated reading course on SAT-V scores. *Personnel and Guidance Journal,* 1967, 46, p. 292-296.

30. Slack, and Porter, The scholastic aptitude test, p. 159.

31. Kroeger, E. Cognitive development in the acculturation of migrant children: The role of training in the assessment of learning ability. *International Review of Applied Psychology,* 1980, 29(1-2), p. 105-118.

32. Bloom, B. *Human Characteristics and School Learning,* New York: McGraw-Hill, 1976.

33. Bell, E. F. Do bar exams serve a useful purpose? *American Bar Association Journal,* 1971, 57, p. 1215-1218.

34. Slack, and Porter, The scholastic aptitude test, p. 179.

Note

There has been some debate regarding the statistical technique employed by Bowles and Gintis. However, their findings are consistent with those of several other studies which demonstrate weak relationships between I.Q., on the one hand, and income, occupational status or quality of performance in particular jobs, on the other.

These studies include:

1. Berg, I. *Education and Jobs: The Great Training Robbery.* Boston: Beacon Press, 1972.
2. Bowles, S. and Nelson, V. The inheritance of I.Q. and intergenerational reproduction of economic inequality. *Review of Economics and Statistics,* 1974, 56(1), p. 39-44.
3. Conslish, J. A bit of evidence on the income-education ability interaction. *Journal of Human Resources,* 1971, 6, p. 358-62.

CHAPTER TEN

WHAT ARE MENTAL TESTS GOOD FOR?

It is here suggested that mental measures of the intellect ought *not* to be used for selection purposes. This because the evidence for validity is too weak to justify making decisions primarily on such a basis. While the tests may not provide a valid vehicle for selection purposes, certain tests such as achievement measures may be of some diagnostic significance and use in planning remedial strategies. General measures of the intellect, however, are notoriously weak with regard to provision of any information pertinent to intervention strategies (1). Perhaps this is not too surprising as intelligence tests have been used most often to meet selection objectives, and hence there has been little refinement with respect to the information they provide regarding underlying cognitive process. This author would argue then that mental measures of the intellect are of value only to the degree that they lead to appropriate teaching efforts and understanding of basic cognitive process.

Another legitimate use of such tests would seem to be as a basis to hold institutions, such as schools, accountable. It was pointed out in Chapter 5 that so-called aptitude measures often reflect the adequacy of the social and educational opportunities provided the individual more so than they do the individual's native intelligence. Jensen and his supporters have, in contrast, deemphasized the institutional determinants of poor performance on standardized aptitude tests. The following section examines this issue in further detail and in the context of recent empirical findings.

113

Mental Measures and Institutional Accountability

Jensen quotes in detail Coleman's (2) study of the effects of schooling upon various populations. He has had reprinted in his text, scores from verbal and nonverbal I.Q. measures taken from Coleman's study which, he claims, accurately reflect ability levels for the minority and Anglo children sampled. The Coleman report concluded that schooling has little effect upon achievement outcome. This argument was based on comparisons between schools with social class controlled. Hence, schools with similar facilities and level of expenditure were compared to each other rather than a comparison being made between poor ghetto schools and affluent suburban schools. Coleman concluded via such a within class comparison process that amount spent on schooling was of little import in affecting student educational attainment. The study provides an interesting case example of how tests, combined with erroneous assumptions, can deflect attention away from the critical institutional determinants of lagging student achievement. Jencks (3), commenting on Coleman's data and similar findings, stated: "Equalizing the quality of high schools would reduce cognitive inequalities by one per cent or less . . . Additional school expenditures are unlikely to increase achievement, and redistributing resources will not reduce test score inequality."

The Coleman study, which initially posited the irrelevance of quality of education in remediating inequities in educational attainment between diverse student groups, has been found faulty by several critics in a number of respects. For instance, Ryan (4) argues that rather than controlling for social class, Coleman ought to have investigated the mechanisms underlying the black-white gap in educational attainment.

With an alternative experimental and statistical design, it would have been possible to control for various aspects of student entry characteristics without at the same time masking the effect of quality of schooling as is discussed in the section on Rutter's work below. Instead, Coleman's study is based upon the à priori assumption that "the larger part of school-to-school variation in achievement appears not to be a consequence of effects of school variations at all but of variations in family backgrounds of entering student bodies" (5, p. 296). The design of his study was then such as to obtain results consistent with the aforementioned assumption upon which it was based.

Rutter (6) discusses additional methodological problems with the Coleman research. Coleman employed a single measure of verbal ability from a standardized intelligence test as the index of educational attainment. Subsequent research demonstrates that such a design leads to an underestimation of the importance of quality of schooling upon attainment. Examined in the next section is Rutter's research on the effects of schooling. His studies have eliminated most of the methodological problems present in the Coleman research.

Rutter's Study on the Effects of Quality of Schooling
Upon Educational Attainment

Rutter compared the progress of children in 12 secondary schools in inner London. Two thousand students were followed up to the end of high school. Rutter found that:

> Although schools differed in the proportion of behaviorally difficult or low achieving children they admitted, these differences did *not* wholly account for the variations between schools in their

pupils' later behavior and attainment. Even when comparisons between schools were restricted to children who were quite similar in family background and personal characteristics prior to secondary transfer, marked school variations remained. The implication is that experiences during the secondary school years may influence children's progress (7, p. 178).

What is more, Rutter found that these significant differences between schools in terms of student achievement levels, rates of delinquency among the student population, and so on were relatively "stable over periods of at least four or five years" (8, p. 178). While Rutter found the physical aspects of schools (i.e., size) not to be of prime importance in producing the differential student outcomes, various social aspects of the school as an institution were significantly related to student achievement levels and behavior (9). The positive social factors included:

(a) *Academic emphasis.* e.g., tendency of teachers to set homework; high teacher academic expectations for greater proportions of their pupils; higher proportions of the school week devoted to teaching as opposed to other activities.

(b) *Teacher behavior during lessons.* e.g., more time devoted by the teacher to the lesson topic as opposed to other activities such as dealing with disciplinary problems; interaction patterns such as the teacher focusing more attention upon the whole class rather than a few individuals.

(c) *Rewards and punishments.* e.g., better academic and behavioral outcomes were associated with discipline based upon general school policy rather than linked to individual teacher style. Rutter suggests that: "The particular rules and approaches to discipline may be less important than the existence of some generally recognized and accepted set of standards" (10, p. 121); various types of rewards tended to be linked with better achievement and behavior.

(d) *Pupil conditions.* e.g., significant correlations between better student outcome and greater willingness of students to approach staff for advice on personal problems were found. Thus, a more pleasant and amiable working environment was positively linked to better achievement levels and fewer behavior problems.

(e) *Responsibilities and participation.* e.g., in schools where more children had some sort of post or responsibility, outcomes were better; schools in which children were given more responsibility to look after school materials and resources also had improved outcome. The student entry characteristics surprisingly did not affect these school process variables significantly (11, p. 179). The ethos of the school then appears to be, in large part, a function of factors other than whether it serves "advantaged" or "disadvantaged" children; the allegedly "bright" or "less bright" (12, p. 27).

Rutter's findings led him to conclude that there is

a strong probability that the associations between school process and outcome reflect in part a *causal* process. In other words, to an appreciable extent, children's behavior and attitudes are shaped and influenced by their experiences at school and, in particular, by the qualities of the school as a social institution (13, p. 179)

Hence, as did Coleman, Rutter found that physical school variables matter little in student outcome. However, unlike the Coleman study, Rutter's work permits that empirically based conclusions be reached regarding the remaining differential in student achievement levels between various groups. While Coleman and Jensen have *speculated* that

117

student entry characteristics are primarily responsible for any variations between schools in terms of student attainment which do exist, Rutter provides empirical evidence that it is instead the social organization of the school itself, in large part, that produces the differences in student outcome between schools. These differences exist even after controlling for children's measured characteristics at intake (14, p. 180-181). Of particular importance is Rutter's finding of a greater correlation between school process variables and children's behavior/attainments at the *end* of secondary schooling. This, Rutter suggests, indicates "a greater effect of schools on children than of children on schools" (15, p. 181). In other words, it is more so the case that schools function as they do not because of the children they admit, but rather that the children come to behave and achieve as they do because of the type of school they attend and the expectations which teachers hold for them. Rutter's work is consistent with many of the propositions advanced by W. Ryan in his text "Blaming the Victim."

Summary

Rutter's research demonstrates the profound effects that school process variables have upon student achievement levels and behavior *independent* of student entry characteristics. This evidence significantly weakens Jensen's (meritocratic) philosophical justifications for the use of aptitude tests in e.g. college selection in that academic promise appears, in large part, institutionally created rather than being the fruition of basic intellect. The use of such tests for selection purposes, it is thus here contended, unfairly penalizes those not exposed to better quality education, some of the characteristics of which have been identified in Rutter's study and in Bloom's work (16).

Given Rutter's findings that the child's cognitive skills are fundamentally altered by school process, it seems reasonable to assume that aptitude test performance is in large part a measure of the effects of that schooling process rather than of the child's native abilities. Consequently, it would seem more justifiable, at this point in the development of psychometrics, to regard aptitude test results as reflections of the quality of the institutional social ethos and the adequacy of the methods of instruction more so than as indicators of the quality or efficiency of individual minds.

Current mental tests, it is here contended, do not provide firm evidence regarding cognitive process, though their use in research for experimental purposes in this regard may be beneficial. Tests which do measure cognitive process would seem a distinct possibility in future, as is discussed in the next chapter.

What has been here argued is that Jensen's claim that mental measures can at present be used to infer properties of the intellect for the making of practical decisions, e.g., college selection, personnel selection is unjustifiable on both empirical and conceptual grounds. In the next chapter process-oriented approaches to the design of mental measures are examined. Some have suggested that such tests *may* hopefully "tell us how the institution should adjust to the person, instead of simply telling us which people are already adjusted to the institution" (17, p. 352).

REFERENCES

1. Wallace, G. and Larsen, S. C. *Educational Assessment of Learning Problems: Testing for Teaching.* Boston: Allyn and Bacon, 1978.
2. Coleman, J. S., et. al. *Equality of Educational Opportunity.* Washington, U.S. Government Printing Office.
3. Jencks, C., et. al. *Inequality: A Reassessment of the Effect of Family and Schooling in America.* New York: Basic Books, 1972.
4. Ryan, W. *Blaming the Victim.* New York: Random House, 1971.
5. Coleman, et. al. *Equality of Educational Opportunity,* p. 296.
6. Rutter, J., Maughan, B., Mortimore, P. and Ouston, J. *Fifteen Thousand Hours: Secondary Schools and Their Effects on Children.* London: Open Books, 1979.
7. Ibid., p. 178.
8. Ibid.
9. Ibid.
10. Ibid., p. 121.
11. Ibid., p. 179.
12. Ibid., p. 27.
13. Ibid., p. 179.
14. Ibid., p. 180-181.
15. Ibid., p. 181.
16. Bloom, B. *Human Characteristics and School Learning.* New York: McGraw-Hill, 1976.
17. Hunt, E., Frost, N. and Lunneborg, C. Cited in Glaser, R. The processes of intelligence and education. In Resnick, L. B. (ed.), *The Nature of Intelligence,* New York: John Wiley and Sons, 1976, p. 341-352.

CHAPTER ELEVEN

RECONCEPTUALIZING THE RELATION BETWEEN MIND AND MENTAL MEASURES

Resnick notes that "the great successes of intelligence testing came . . . when pretenses of measuring 'basic' or 'underlying' processes were dropped" (1, p. 4). Jensen, as with other meritocratic philosophers, did not relinquish the notion of mental measures of aptitude as tapping basic cognitive process. Due to advances in cognitive research, there has been a renewed interest and optimism among others than simply the meritocratic philosophers regarding the possibility of designing mental measures which are more clearly process-oriented. Such tests, it is hoped, would have more specific treatment implications than is currently the case with general measures of intelligence and aptitude. Many argue that: "It would be a useful contribution to develop techniques for sorting out groups of individuals suitable for . . . specified kinds of treatment" (2, p. 23-24).

The potential negative social impacts involved in selection based upon process-oriented mental measures will no doubt become painfully obvious once such a testing movement gets underway. For the purposes of this discussion the focus is, however, upon what changes in conceptualization must be effected to bring about a testing industry better informed by the findings of cognitive and other areas of psychological research, as well as by work in the field of artificial intelligence. The question arises as to whether, as Voss argues:

One may keep mental testing, but if it is kept, it must be refined —

perhaps beyond recognition (and possibly beyond recall) . . . it must be re-evaluated in the light of the advancements of experimental psychology and of the concerns regarding cultural interactions (3, p. 314).

The Notion of General Intelligence and
Process-Oriented Mental Measures

In Voss' view, the development of process-oriented mental measures will not rid the fields of psychometrics and experimental psychology of the debate over the validity and value of general measures of intelligence (4, p. 315). It is here argued that an emphasis upon process-oriented mental measures will nevertheless eventually necessitate a rejection of the notion of general intelligence in that cognitive research simply does not support the viability of such a concept. The research of Kail (5) and Stevenson et. al. (6) is particularly pertinent to this issue. These investigators have provided suggestive evidence which weakens the notion of a "general memory ability" or even a general competence for formulating "memory strategies."

Stevenson et. al. (7) tested 255 five year olds on eleven different memory tasks including digit span, recall of stories, and recall of pictures. When the measures were intercorrelated, less than half of the relationships found were significant. Similar findings were reported in a study by Kail (8) with 100 eight and nine year olds. For both, the younger and older subject samples, average correlations obtained were in the order of .18. Studies concerned with "general strategic ability" have produced similar results. Kail (9) tested the notion of such a general strategic ability with eight and nine year olds, using three memory tasks requiring the use of various mnemonic strategies. For the eight year olds no significant correlations were found among the strategy-based measures of memory functioning. Findings with the eleven year olds revealed significant but quite small correlations (r= .28, r= .44). Kail was led to conclude that: "General strategic ability is not a source of individual difference among eight year olds and only a moderate source of variation among eleven year olds" (10, p. 106).

Given that memory processes are thought to be a critical aspect of intellectual functioning, and that cognitive research findings do not point to a general memory component, it would appear unlikely that process-oriented mental measures would delineate a general intelligence factor. It is here suggested that the alleged general intelligence factor derived from certain current mental measures is an artifact of the test construction rather than a reflection of the properties of mind. The intercorrelations among a set of tests do not at all necessarily point to the existence of a general intelligence factor, contrary to the claims of Cooley (11). Rather, this general factor may, as has been alluded to previously, reflect general skills for dealing with decontextualized material which for problem-solution requires a particular "schooled" logic. This author is in accord with Voss that "the concept of general intelligence is a remnant of faculty psychology" (12, p. 315).

Estes points out that there has been a gradual abandonment by many psychologists of the notion that "intercorrelations and factor analyses would lead to uncovering the basic structure of the mind" (13, p. 297). The concept of general intelligence and the strategies for examining "intellectual" strengths and deficiencies it has fostered have been less than fruitful in terms of furthering understanding of basic cognitive process. The à priori assumption has been that current mental measures assess something of great import with regard to intellectual process when, in fact, there is no independent evidence to suggest precisely what form of mental activity the items (tasks) on such tests evoke. It is to be hoped that similar unfounded assumptions do not hinder a process-oriented mental testing approach. Estes cautions against "simply identifying cognitive processes involved in intellectual tasks (and) the supposition that these processes are automatically called forth in the presence of tests in other situations" (14, p. 279).

On the Potential for Re-inventing the Wheel Using Process-Oriented Mental Measures

Hunt states "It is the business of psychology to provide some hints about how we can ensure that information presented does indeed get into the head, how it is organized when it gets there, and how it can be fetched upon demand" (15, p. 309). Process-oriented mental measures, it is suggested here, may better assess the strategies individuals use to transform the input as Hunt describes. At present, so-called general measures of intelligence assess only the ability to produce a particular product and not the process underlying that output. Whether these underlying processes are efficient high level functions or the reverse, current aptitude tests provide no evidence on this point.

Tasks which do provide insights into basic cognitive process already exist and are commonly used by cognitive researchers. These tasks would seem to offer a promising base for development of mental measures which provide qualitative data about modes of information processing. For example, process-oriented memory tasks have been used to *infer* types of memory search strategies such as the serial exhaustive scan (16); the number of scanning and comparison processes used to solve a problem (17) and so on. Hunt argues that such tasks have the potential to measure something of the mechanisms underlying differences in intelligence. He cites, for instance, a study which demonstrated negative correlations on the order of $r=-.34$ between scores on a verbal reasoning test and reaction time on a task requiring recall of varying numbers of facts. Hunt concludes from such findings that "verbal intelligence is related to the speed of information processing . . . (and) our . . . performance . . . on the intelligence test, is an amalgamation of knowledge and information processing *capacity*" (18, p. 321). Once again then the notion of structural variables (capacity limitations) is highlighted rather than a view of intellectual process as dynamic. The concept of general intelligence is placed in a new research context but differs not in substance. General intelligence conceived of as information processing capacity is, in a sense, an attempt at re-inventing the wheel. Such a view loses much of what is novel and valuable about a process-oriented approach to the design of mental measures. The relationship between information processing tasks such as are used in cognitive research and intelligence test performance suggests that intelligence tests are, in effect, assessing the adequacy of the individual's cognitive strategies for transforming and utilizing input at a particular point in his developmental history. Intelligence tests, however, involve heterogeneous items, many of which are selected with no conceptual justification but rather on the basis of their ability to differentiate between individuals: "Most aptitude test items are selected on the basis of their predictive power in our rather uniform educational programs rather than on their relationship to observed or hypothesized intellectual processes . . . " (19, p. 33). Consequently,

125

little understanding of the nature of such learning strategies has yet been derived from them: "attempts to relate different learning strategies to different patterns of primary mental abilities or factor scores have generally been unsuccessful" (20, p. 24).

There seems then to be a strong residual group of psychologists and psychometricians favoring the notion of general intelligence conceived either in familiar terms or ineffectively disguised in terms of information-processing terminology. Perhaps this is so because genuinely process-oriented mental measures would be shown to be highly task-specific. One could infer from such measures only information processing limitations as they apply to a *particular* task, given the strategies available to the individual at a particular time, and with the particular training he had received. Insofar as various tasks differ in terms of the cognitive demands they make and the processes they trigger, no inference about general capacity can be reasonably made. Hunt, in drawing a distinction between information processing capacity and strategy is, it is here contended, inadvertently rejecting the essence of a process-oriented view. Hunt states: "Information processing involves more than a capacity, it involves a strategy" (21, p. 323). The value of the process-oriented view is that it teaches that capacity and strategy are, in fact, inseparable. Capacity will expand as efficient cognitive strategies are acquired. Capacity then is dynamic.

The limits to cognitive modifiability are as yet undefined and cannot be adequately delineated by general intelligence tests as indicated, for instance, by the continually changing conceptions of what processing capabilities the retarded possess. Indeed, many in the field of retardation hold that no reliable expectations of any specificity can be made about the retarded individual's performance on the basis of psychometric tests. Training subjects in strategy use has, for instance, been found to improve performance significantly as was discussed in Chapter 6. Jensen's Level I and Level II abilities would, according to this view, appear to represent differing information processing capacity levels reflecting strategy availability and use. Capacity may also expand due to the spontaneity with which available strategies are accessed.

Case suggests, for instance, that:

> The gradual increase in working memory does not stem from a structural increase in the capacity of the organism but rather from an increase in the automaticity of the basic operations it is capable of executing. As these operations become more automatic, their execution requires a smaller proportion of total attentional capacity. The result is that more capacity is available for "storage" or "working" (22, p. 65).

The data presented previously regarding development of strategy use in the mentally retarded appear to be consistent with Case's proposition. One of the major factors underlying the mentally retarded individual's memory problems is his passive response to tasks and failure to call up strategies when available.

Assessments of capacity in isolation, out of the developmental and situational context, are not possible. Current general measures of intelligence claim to accomplish just this — that is an assessment of global capacity which is not task or situation specific, for instance. In actuality, however, such measures reflect the efficiency of the individual's information-processing skills at any particular point in time given a particular learning history and current assessment situation. It would seem that the demand for global measures of the intellect, assessments of general capacity, is linked to the motive to rationalize and legitimize selection procedures. There would seem to be little empirical evidence to suggest that the notion of "general abilities" which cut across qualitatively different intellectual tasks is a viable one.

On a different question — that of the role of personality variables in intellectual behavior — process-oriented perspectives have much to offer. Such variables have typically been neglected in the context of traditional approaches to intellectual assessment. Koran states, and this author concurs: "Information processing models could conceivably be used in analyzing the influences of individual differences in noncognitive variables on cognitive processes involved in problem solving" (23, p. 332). Koran cites as an example of such a contribution, a study (24) demonstrating that the negative performance consequences arising from excessive anxiety are mediated by their effects upon short-term memory. Providing short-term memory supports was found to be especially effective for highly anxious learners. Information processing approaches to the examination and assessment of intellectual behavior thus potentially promise (if the unfounded biases of the past are relinquished) an analysis of cognitive skills which is at once more comprehensive and diagnostically relevant. Whether such a perspective will also lead to a more humane use of mental measures is a question which is considerably more difficult to speculate upon. This will largely depend upon the ideological framework in which it is embedded.

REFERENCES

1. Resnick, L. B. Introduction: Changing conceptions of intelligence. In Resnick, L. B. (ed.), *The Nature of Intelligence.* New York: John Wiley and Sons, 1976, p. 1-10.

2. Tyler, L. E. The intelligence We Test: An evolving concept. In Resnick, *The Nature of Intelligence,* p. 13-26.

3. Voss, J. F. The nature of "The Nature of Intelligence." In Resnick, *Nature of Intelligence,* p. 307-315.

4. Ibid., p. 315.

5. Kail, R. *The Development of Memory in Children.* San Francisco: W. H. Freeman and Co., 1979, p. 103-126.

6. Stevenson, H. W., Parker, T. and Wilkinson, A. Ratings and measures of memory processes in young children, Unpublished manuscript, University of Michigan, 1975.

7. Ibid.

8. Kail, *The Development of Memory in Children,* p. 103-126.

9. Ibid.

10. Ibid.

11. Cooley, W. W. Who needs general intelligence. In Resnick, L. B. (ed.), *Nature of Intelligence,* p. 57-61.

12. Voss, The Nature of "The Nature of Intelligence," p. 307-315.

13. Estes, W. K. Intelligence and cognitive psychology. In Resnick, L. B., *Nature of Intelligence,* p. 295-305.

14. Ibid., p. 299.

15. Hunt, E. We know who knows, but why? In Anderson, R. C., Spiro, R. J. and Montague, W. E. (eds.) *Schooling and the Acquisition of Knowledge,* New York: John Wiley & Sons, p. 309-325.

16. Sternberg, S. High speed scanning in human memory. *Science,* 1966, 153, p. 652-654.

17. Carpenter, P. and Just, M. Sentence comprehension: A psycholinguistic model of verification. *Psychological Review,* 1975, 82, p. 45-73.

18. Hunt, We know who knows, but why? p. 309-325.

19. Koran, M. L. Individual differences in information processing. In Anderson, R. C., Spiro, R., and Montague, W. E. (eds.) *Schooling,* p. 327-333.

20. Tyler, L. E. The intelligence We Test, p. 13-26.

21. Hunt, We know who knows, but why? p. 309-325.

22. Case, R. Intellectual Development from Birth to Adulthood: A Neo-Piagetian Interpretation. In Siegler, R. S. (ed.), *Children's Thinking: What Develops?* Hillsdale: Lawrence Erlbaum, 1978.

23. Koran, Individual differences in information processing, p. 327-333.

24. Sieber, J. E. A paradigm for experimental modification of the effects of test anxiety on cognitive process. *American Educational Research Journal,* 1969, 6, p. 46-61.

CONCLUDING REMARKS

INADVERTENT LESSONS DERIVED FROM THE
MENTAL TESTING MOVEMENT

The psychometric testing movement has highlighted the fact that quantification need not necessarily be linked to conceptual refinement, a point I have made also elsewhere (1). Like Blum, this author argues that the modern psychometric endeavor includes its share of "fallacies, exaggerations and false claims" (2, p. 68). As with other paradigms in science, such exaggerations and premature claims are difficult to eliminate for scientists are often reluctant to dispense with particular conceptual notions and assumptions, despite disconfirmatory evidence (3). That many such unfounded claims have been widely accepted by both scientist and nonscientist is a lesson both in the sociology and philosophy of science. This phenomenon suggests that scientific models and notions consistent with dominant public values and "common sense" presumptions tend to be regarded as viable regardless of the empirical findings. Thus, the I.Q. test is regarded (falsely) by many as a valuable tool for assessing intellectual capacity and potential despite the absence of empirical evidence suggesting that current psychometric measures do either adequately[1]. The tests serve the public demand for *apparently* justifiable selection procedures and criteria and, hence, the claims made for the tests are not often carefully scrutinized.

The psychometric movement provides a case example of the fact that measuring devices are essentially theoretical in nature regardless of the statistical data they generate. Mental measures are not neutral means for assessing individual differences, as Jensen claims, but rather interpretive frameworks which may emphasize differences of

131

little import, while they mask others. Often they provide individual profiles composed of hypothetical abilities (factors) derived from performance on tasks which measure processes of which the tester is ignorant, and whose significance to an understanding of basic cognitive process remains to be determined.

The psychometric tradition demonstrates how close the links are between pseudo-science and science. This author, unlike Blum, does not, however, argue that psychometrics is inherently a pseudo-scientific endeavor. The difficulties in distinguishing between pseudo-science and science have been outlined by Cooter (4). Cooter argues that it is inappropriate to regard psychometrics as a pseudo-science, on the grounds that it is infiltrated by meritocratic ideology (as does Blum) for there is "out there (no) real, objective (non-ideological) body of truth called Science" (5, p. 240). One is led to concur with Cooter that the charge levelled against psychometrics of being inherently pseudo-scientific serves to reinforce the kind of positivistic philosophy of science which permits those such as Jensen to claim that I.Q. tests measure "real" differences of significance between persons, differences which are not importantly related to the design of the tests themselves. This author rejects what might be termed "scientific realism" (6); a realism as evidenced in the sweeping claims made by Jensen and his supporters regarding the power of mental measures and the meaning of the data they generate. While the psychometric tradition is not *intrinsically* pseudo-scientific, to the extent that the meritocratic philosophers, and the psychometricians among them, claim to have created mental measures which are more than but assumptions and theoretical models of the human intellect, both of which are open to question, these investigators are engaging in pseudo-science. Here follows a quote which perhaps both sides of the I.Q. controversy would do well to keep in mind in the debate on the nature of the intellect and how best to assess it.

Men who have excessive faith in their theories are not only ill prepared for making discoveries; they also make very poor observations. Claude Bernard (7).

REFERENCES

1. Grover, S. C. Implications of quantification in psychological research and educational practice. *Interchange,* 1977-78, 8(3), p. 70-71.
2. Blum, J. M. *Pseudoscience and Mental Ability: The Origins and Fallacies of the I.Q. Controversy.* New York: Monthly Review Press, 1978.
3. Barber, B. Resistance by scientists to scientific discovery. *Science,* 1961, 134, p. 596-602.
4. Cooter, R. Deploying 'pseudoscience': then and now. In Hanen, M. P., Osler, M. J., and Weyant, R. G. (eds.) *Science, Pseudo-Science and Society,* Waterloo: Wilfred Laurier University Press, 1980.
5. Cooter, Deploying 'Pseudoscience': Then and Now, p. 240.
6. Grover, S. C. *Toward a Psychology of the Scientist: Implications of Psychological Research for Contemporary Philosophy of Science,* University Press of America, Lanham (in press).
7. Bernard, C. *An Introduction to the Study of Experimental Medicine* (Original 1865) New York: Dover, 1957.

NOTE

1. Jensen claims that the concepts of "capacity" and "potential" are no longer a part of modern psychometrics. He contends that these notions have been replaced by "conditional probability statements about the individual's genotypic value on the trait. . . . measured by the test" (i, p. 243). Such probability statements make use of the notion of the "heritability" of test scores, a concept which has been severely criticized by Kamin among others. Nevertheless, the use of I.Q. tests for selection purposes perpetuates the view that intellectual capacity and potential can be assessed "scientifically". It seems unjustifiable to make selection decisions using mental tests which, by Jensen's own admission, "measure what the individual can do at the time of taking the test and not . . . . what he *could* do under some other conditions or at some future time" (2, p. 242).

REFERENCES

I. Jensen, A.R. *Bias in Mental Testing.* New York: The Free Press, 1980,   p. 243.
2. Jensen, *Bias in Mental Testing*, p.242.

ABOUT THE AUTHOR

Sonja C. Grover is also author of *A Manual for the Analysis of Human Behavior in the Psychological Laboratory* (in press) and *Toward a Psychology of the Scientist: Implications of Psychological Research for Contemporary Philosophy of Science* (in press). Before attending graduate school, she spent a year at the Psychology Department, University of Sussex, England, working as a research assistant. She received her M.A. from Lakehead University, Ontario, in 1973 and Ph.D. from the University of Toronto in 1976. After receiving her doctorate, she was an educational researcher with University of Toronto while also teaching part-time at Nipissing University. She has been Assistant Professor at the Faculty of Education, Queen's University, Ontario, and at the Department of Psychology, Lakehead University. Subsequently she assumed the position of senior psychologist with Alberta Mental Health and taught a course in psychoeducational assessment at the University of Alberta. Currently she is on the faculty at the Department of Educational Psychology at the University of Calgary, Alberta. She has published articles in various areas including language disorder, inferential thought processes, word recognition, and moral development. She is presently collaborating on a book for educators dealing with cognitive process.

AUTHOR INDEX

9937